The Poetry of Alexander Anderson

Alexander Anderson was born on April 30th 1845 in Kirkconnel, Dumfries and Galloway, Scotland, the sixth and youngest son of James Anderson, a quarrier.

When he was three, the family moved to Crocketford in Kirkcudbrightshire where he attended the local school. Years later Anderson would take long walks in the surrounding hills finding inspiration for his poetry from both the stunning landscape and its local reputation for martyrdom.

At 16 he was back in his native village working in a quarry. Two years after that, in 1862, he switched careers to the railways becoming a surfaceman or platelayer on the Glasgow and South-western railway. He now used 'Surfaceman' as his pseudonym.

Anderson is recognised as one of Scotland's leading poets and, as a young man, he spent much time learning languages such as French, German and Spanish well enough so that he could immerse himself in their poetry and better the quality of his own.

By 1870 he was sending poems to 'The People's Friend' of Dundee.

In 1873 his first book, 'A Song of Labour and other Poems', was published by the Dundee Advertiser in a print run of 1000. With the support of The People's Friend the run sold out within two weeks.

The Rev George Gilfillan, a poetry critic in Dundee, was also effusive in his praise. He wrote to Thomas Aird saying: "You will be greatly interested in his simple manner and appearance—an unspoiled Burns is these respects and not without a little real mens divinor. Of course you know his poetry and his remarkable history".

Examples of his poems were also published in the many of the time's leading periodicals Good Words, Chambers's Journal, Cassell's Magazine, Fraser's Magazine and the Contemporary Review.

It was a good decade for him. Other poetry volumes were also published: 'Two Angels' (1875), 'Songs of the Rail' (1878), and 'Ballads and Sonnets' (1879).

In the following year he was made assistant librarian in the University of Edinburgh, and after an interval as secretary to the Philosophical Institution, which he seemed not to enjoy, he returned as Chief Librarian to the University.

Anderson would write no further volumes but would still occasionally contribute to periodicals and magazines.

Alexander Anderson died at his home in Edinburgh on 11th July 1909 at age 64.

He left behind a number of unpublished poems which were collected and published as 'Later Poems' in 1912

Index of Contents

I

This, with the memory of that sweet day,
When all the placid dreamings of each hill
Were deep within us, and the thoughts that fill
And widen out our being, as the grey
Morning unfolds itself before the light.
For at our feet, and all between us two,
Lay the pure grave of Wordsworth in our view,
All green and dewy with the tears of night.
We felt as if the spirit of the place
Were with us. We were one with all sweet things—
Stream, hill, and lake, had each their tender claim
To proffer, and their voices, like the strings
Of some great harp, were sounding forth one name;
While nature knelt and look'd up in our face.

II

Our old life fled, and, like a thing forgot,
Lay with the yesterdays that make the past,
While over all, like purer light, was cast
The placid consecration of the spot.
And as a mother leads with winning speech
The footsteps of her child, so he who still
Remains the poet priest of stream and hill,
Led us away into the higher reach
Where spirit touches spirit, till we saw
A newer meaning on the very grass,
Whose freshness was the colour of his art,
A glory in mute things, a sacred awe
Of some high end in all that is and was,
And still he kept his hand upon our heart.

III

And so I give, in token of that hour,
This simple book of early song to thee,
Sung in far years that had a richer dower,
And brought twelve Mays instead of one to me,
The gift is nothing—for to me it seems
Mere spindrift from those mighty waves of song,
Heard in my youth, as sailors hear in dreams,
The booming of the sullen ocean, strong

For conflict with the shore.   But thou and I
Can only feel the link that lies in This,—
The interchange of thought, the quiet bliss,
And all the silent rapture of the sky,
While at our feet, as earnest of that trust,
Which is of faith and love—the poet's dust.

IN ROME, A POEM IN SONNETS

I

Tomorrow I will be in Rome, and thou
Within thy village.   I can see thee stand,
Thine eyes in the direction of this land:
Fair pillar of the past, as it is now
The refuge of its heirlooms.   In my ears
I hear thee speaking as upon that day
We parted, saying—"When thou goest away
To make a golden epoch in thy years
By travel, speak not of the Rhine's swift roll,
Mont Blanc, the Jungfrau, or the Alps that rise
Like icy Titans, nor of sunset skies;
But when thou reachest Rome let all thy soul
Fly to the past, and as it speaks to thee
From out its temples, speak thou so to me."

II

The one dream of our boyhood!   Dost thou not
Remember how we stood in mimic fight,
And marshall'd all our legion's puny might,
Then fann'd ourselves to ardour fierce and hot?
"Thus struck a Roman for his Rome!" we cried—
"Thus, thus into the gulf a Curtius leapt!"
And with a sudden shout and rush we swept
The foe back, till they fled on every side.
Then came the hymn of triumph, and the car
Bearing the victor to the feast and wine,
And the delights of smiling peace and home;
All this was with me of that mimic war,
As I pass'd through the arch of Constantine,
And stood within the centuries and Rome!

III

If thou have, for the weak, defenceless past
Aught in thee like to reverence, be dumb,
And speak not, but let thought and feeling come
As mourners, and in kindred silence cast
Their sorrow on this city, now no more
The foreground of the world, but lying dead,
While the great present with its hasty tread
Moves on, and turns not save but to deplore.
The background of our Planet! But in death
She hath that awe which broods upon the face
Of the new dead, so in her fallen place
A power is with her still, though all her faith
Is snapt like her own temples in the dust,
And fades with centuries of age and rust.

IV

I am in Rome, and underneath the spell
Of her past glory; as I tread her streets,
My soul keeps saying, as a child repeats
Its lesson—"The Eternal, here they dwell!"
I am alone, though in the busy crowd,
Yet mighty spirits keep their pace with mine:
Horace and Virgil, and those names divine
That in the world for ever speak aloud.
The past is with me, and my eyes are blind
To all the modern change on either side;
I stride a Roman, with a Roman's stride,
And feel a Roman's firmness fire my mind.
I even hail the victor from afar,
And join the throng that shout behind his car.

V

Yet after all, when the soul finds its home,
And we look with our daily eyes, we ask
(Doubt round us like a mist) "Can this be Rome?"
And the slow answer is a mighty task.
Can this indeed be Rome, who from her heart
Sent shocks of life, like blood, through distant
lands.

Whose Kings were sons to her by Roman bands
Of valour, and their tribute fill'd her mart?
The Jupiter of cities!   Now, alas!
Upon her throne of seven hills, she seems
The shadow of a thousand former dreams,
Pointing to all the splendid pomp that was.
Even her columns seem to start and glow
Into Cassandras, and wail forth her woe.

VI

Where'er thou stand in ancient Rome there seems
A shadow with thee; and if thy keen thought
Turn pilgrim to the shrine of thy great dreams—
Paying continual homage as it ought—
Thou art but fool'd; and if thou rear again
Columns and gods and temples, and within
The silent Forum place her mightiest men,
Whose eloquence could calm and still the din
Of factions, lo! the Presence at thy side
Cries, "Siste, viator," and from out the past
Thy soul comes, and instead of all the pride
And high magnificence that was, thou hast,
Like garments of the mighty flung away,
Marbles and columns in one mix'd decay.

VII

What high, great thoughts might leap within the breast
Of the stern Romulus, that day when he
Ran a light furrow round his Rome to be,
Built huts, and, for a moment, took his rest.
Would he had been a Capys then, and seen,
From the rude doorway, all the splendid power
Taking still birth from out that quiet hour,
And spreading like a shadow all between
The earth and sky, until its mighty wings
Were at full stretch, and a great empire stood
Flinging steel network over earthly things,
Till, tired of uncheck'd force and constant blood,
Turn'd like the Titans, when it thus had striven,
And dared to parcel out the rights of heaven.

VIII

I saw the mighty form of giant Time!
He stood; within his hands were balances:
He held them up; two kingdoms were in these;
One sunk; the other rose and flower'd to prime.
Around his feet his sons, the young, keen years,
Wrestled and shaped fresh worlds; as they shaped
They look'd up; through their lips a moan escaped,
And in their eyes was something, like to tears.
Then with one voice they cried—"Is not the hour
Ready? Put down thy balances, and lift
The nations we have foster'd as a gift
For thee." And Time, frowning till eyebrows met,
Shook his white locks in sternly potent power,
Then whisper'd back to them—"Not yet, not yet!"

IX

St. Peter's! how thy soul within thee grows
And widens out in worship, as if God
Had made this dome a moment His abode;
Then left His awful shadow to repose
Within its walls for ages. Let no speech,
Or aught of earth be with thee, in this hour
When the full past falls, like a sudden shower
Upon thee, bringing into all thy reach
The sacredness of what it hallows, till
Thou standest not on marble but on air,
Feeling thyself uplifted by the will
Of some great Presence dwelling everywhere;
Then, looking up, see right before thine eyes
God's very threshold to the bending skies.

X

The first brief hour within the Vatican
Is one in which thy soul can find no speech;
But dumbly yearns to gain those points to which
Climb the great possibilities of man.
Frescoes, mosaics, statues! all that speaks
Of the creative and refining power—
God's share in man,—that ever like a dower

Falls on him, and in fruitful silence seeks
High forms to build it forth, is here; and we,
Who pilgrimage to all our greater kind,
Know not the force that leads us, but must bow
Before the eternal Roman sway of mind,
Blind with the same clear light which now I see
Upon the beautiful Meleager's s brow.

XI

To shape, when the pure thought was high and free,
Some mighty god, that, ever as we look,
We feel its godhead with a stern rebuke
Claim worship, and we almost bend the knee—
This is the task of those grand souls who stand
A thousand years between them; for the given
Fire, burning at the very core of heaven,
Cannot be flung broadcast from out the hand;
But where it lights, ay, there it ever burns,
A clear flame on the ember'd hearth of Time,
Quenchless but with himself. Lo! how it turns
From the high Greek and all his higher glow,
And, shooting onward to a sister clime,
Crowns with no stint a later Angelo.

XII

The thoughts that only mate with gods alone
And all that high conception when the mind
Looks heavenward for a model to its kind
Of what a god may be, meet here in stone.
The Sun God! Dost thou not behold him now
With head thrown back, as if his native sky
Had come, in some wild moment, all too nigh,
Then fled, but left its splendours on his brow?
Thou glorious Archer! In that awful hour,
Granted by Heaven, did the sculptor kneel
Before his chisel touch'd the virgin block,
Feeling thy presence give consent and power?
We know not. We can only see and feel
That Heaven's fire with his sped every stroke.

XIII

Back to the grand Apollo! Tell me not
A mortal had to do with this. I know
That if a god content him here below,
A mightier one must bind him to the spot.
Can this be genius that can so enthral,
And lift us, Mahomet-like, until we feel
The very heaven around us, and we reel
In the delight of worship? Who can call
This splendid triumph stone? Say rather we
Behold a god who came to men, and met
His punishment in marble; yet he lives
While we, with all our throbbing being set,
Worship with the bold thought that it may be
Idolatry that Heaven itself forgives.

XIV

I turn'd from the Apollo with my mind
Back to the Venus. I can see her now
Looking at me with that divine-like brow
Round which the adoring world will ever bind
Its love for ages. All that hath been sung
Since Time grew up to manhood lingers round
That snowy form, that ever seems spell-bound
In its own whiteness, and for ever young.
We lose our being as we look and wear
Into her beauty, and become as naught;
We are the stone, and she the glowing thought,
For ever with us and for ever fair,—
Goddess of Love—and we who stand but seem
To touch the confines of her endless dream!

XV

I see her yet—the glorious shape to which
The pilgrim fondly wanders! Let me kneel,
As if in that one act my soul could feel
And, all miraculously lifted, reach
The sculptor's height in that impassion'd hour
When the fair dream the world will not let die
Took shape in stone, as if a god were nigh,
Limb, breast, and brow asserting conscious power

And claiming worship. O! did she look thus
In that sweet hour, when glowing from her flight
She knelt by pale Endymion in delight,
Kissing his brow and lip, and tremulous
With sighs from heaven, whisper, "It is he,
The Latmian!"—and so let her passion free.

XVI

I stood before the Laocoön, and felt
A soul move in the stone; as if the pain
For ever prison'd there had power to melt
And fuse itself in double strength again
Into the gazer as he stands, and feels
The marble horror catch his breath until
He sinks, and, in his very weakness, reels
Before that form those coilings never kill.
Look on the father who with quivering form
Strives to unlace the strain that never slips,
But keeps eternal clasp upon the place
While all the agony, like a lake in storm,
Moves from huge limbs to straining finger tips,
Then makes a dread Vesuvius of the face.

XVII

Temple of all the gods! and here the dust
Of one reposes, who with early fame
Went into death, and left behind the name
Of Raphael, to defy the years' quick rust.
How shall we name him who with quick, pure eyes
Saw Heaven's Divinest, and in earth-made hues
Painted the glory of His look, as dews
Catch the first light that falls from summer skies?
Say, poet of Christ in colours, who stood near
The light of Heaven, until its very strength
Took him all kindly to itself at length,
Yet left him not, but went before his bier,
And, soul like in that work, his last and best,
Saw the great Master enter into rest.

XVIII

The stone rolls from His feet like mountain mist;
Before Him, ghost-like, in the vanquish'd tomb,
The bands of linen lie within the gloom—
White pledges of the newly-risen Christ.
He comes forth! from the splendour of His brow
Gethsemane and the Cross have fled.   He stands,
A halo of love around Him, as His hands
Clasp each in prayer; God's early morning glow
Falls on Him, matching in those deep, sad eyes
The light of conquest gain'd for all our race,
As if God bent Himself, and from above
Shed on Him all the glory of the skies;
While the earth, dumb at such astounding love;
Turns round to gaze for ever on His face.

XIX

Here on this spot the heroic martyr stood,
God's fire upon his brow and in his heart,
As the two gladiators drew apart
Glaring at each in their wild thirst for blood.
Lo! as the ages roll aside their gloom
We see him yet; the hero as he sinks
Keeps to his purpose born of Christ, nor shrinks
Though human tigers track him to his doom.
Talk of this planet's holy spots! my feet
Within this amphitheatre are on
Its holiest, for a brother here alone
Stood up for God and man, till in the heat
Of Roman thirst for blood he sank, and pass'd,
An early Livingstone, but not the last.

XX

I saw the stage of Time, and on it kings
Strutted and fought, then laid them on the bed
Of earth, that took them, like the blood they shed,
Kindly; and they were with forgotten things.
Then nations rose, who, branching out became
The very backbone of the universe.
They reach'd their bloom until, as when a curse
Withers, they shrank and dwindled like a flame
That lacks fresh fuel.   All this while I saw

Shadows creep o'er their ruins, and in awe
I turn'd to Time, and ask'd him to define
These shadows; and he answer'd thus to me—
"These are the forecasts of great worlds to be;"
I woke, and I was on the Palatine.

XXI

Are nations, then, like flowers that have their bloom,
Dying, as the still centuries pass away?
Alas! behind their acmè lurks the doom
To write its "Mene" on corroding clay.
Belief, whether it be in gods or God,
Can still work miracles; but if it fail,
And Argus doubt with poisonous darts assail
Its inmost hold; then realms and men corrode.
The Past behind thee teaches this.   Look back!
Lo! from the wreck of worlds stand Greece and Rome
With pleading silence in their eyes, whose track
Shows what may be when doubt has found a home.
I stood in Rome, but, when this came to me,
My England!   I was looking back to thee.

XXII

Two of great England's singers, lying each
By each: one rose up wroth at human wrong,
And hung half-way to heaven in his song,
Till the heart burst in his desire to teach
The melody he heard from where he was.
The other wander'd to the early past,
Yearning with a boy's ardour to recast
Its mythologic utterances.   But as
The sun takes dews, so did their beauty him;
He pass'd, leaving behind sweet words that must
For ever keep him here.   The other, too,
Left melody that still will float and swim;
Aerial mist with heaven shining through,
And here a little space divides their dust.

XXIII

Cor Cordium, thou art near to Shelley's heart;
Stop, if thou canst, the beatings of thine own,
For here a purer beats a perfect part,
And models thought upon a purer tone.
Ay, Shelley's heart, it may be naught to thee,
But in it lay the light which, though unseen,
Had the full stamp of that which is to be—
It now is, but the earth is all between.
I claim no tears for him.   If thou art one
Who hears between the breathing of the years,
Thou shalt not miss his music; if alone,
It shall be sweeter and seem from the spheres;
For his was from the higher realm of good
Brought down to men, not to be understood.

XXIV

And wilt thou go away from Rome, nor see
The resting-place of Keats, from whom thy soul
Took early draughts of worship and control—
A pilgrim thou, and from beyond the sea?
I turn'd, and stood beside his grassy grave,
Almost within the shadow of the wall
Honorian; and as kindred spirits call
Each unto each, my own rose up to crave
A moment's sweet renewal by the dust
Of that high interchange in vanish'd time,
When my young soul was reeling with his prime;
But now my manhood lay across that trust.
Ah! had I stood here in my early years,
This simple headstone had been wet with tears.

XXV

I go, for wider is the space that lies
Between the sleeper in his grave and me;
I look back on my golden youth, but he
Cannot look backward with less passion'd eyes.
There is no change in him; the fading glory
Of mighty Rome's long triumph is around.
But cannot come anear or pierce the bound
Of this our laurell'd sleeper, whose pale story
Takes fresher lustre with the years that fly.
But Roman dust upon an English heart

Is naught, yet this is Keats's, and a part
Of England's spirit. With a weary sigh
I turn from sacred ground, and all the way
Two spirits were with me —Keats and David Gray.

XXVI

I left the crowd to its own will, and mused
Upon thy village life, that scarcely opes
One pathway for the liberal thought, nor copes
With the result that broadens; but suffused
With straiten'd range of thought, keeps on, nor sees
The world with proper vision. Creeds and sects
Are here, still seeing within each defects,
And men will battle to the last for these.
It will be so. Yet think, ere we condemn,
What our faith is to us is theirs to them;
And so grow broad with sympathy, nor sink
Into the barren pasture of old saws,
But think that God will open up His laws,
And tell us we are safer than we think.

XXVII

Tiber! thy city's great have sunk and died
Making her famous, yet thou rollest on
(For time shrinks back from nature); in thy tone
To me, a pilgrim standing by thy side,
A threnody comes forth and fills my ears;
And all the heroic annals of the past
Rise up, as if the hand of time had cast
Its fingers on the keyboard of the years,
Hymning their changes. What a mighty reach
From the wild, fierce, wolf-suckled twins until
Seven hills saw mighty Rome repose on each—
Gateway to worlds which she oped at will,
But now for ever shut, and in her ken
No "sesame" to open them again!

XXVIII

Tiber! before I pass away from thee,

One other dream. I stand with half-shut eye,
And hear a mighty army's vaunt and cry;
Then see within the pass the heroic Three.
Hark to the clang that strikes against the bridge
That shakes (such strength was in a Roman's blow,
When faith was potent centuries ago);
Then the loud crash, as two from off its ledge
Leap among friends. But where is he, the best,
The mightiest—Horatius? In thy wave
He plunges, and around him thou dost lave
Thy yellow surges on his mailèd breast.
Thy foam is on his beard, he gains the land,
Thou Roman! and I stretch him forth my hand.

XXIX

Who rests within this soil must slumber well,
For on it the sad, earnest past hath shed
Its holiest consecration, and the dead
Know it, and beneath can feel its spell;
To die, then, and to rest in Roman mould
Were something: wearing into all the past,
Whose glory like a sunbeam backward cast
Might keep the heart from ever growing cold.
It is as if the spirit of ancient Rome
Unveiling all its glory, cried—"Come ye
And look upon me, but in looking die,
And let thy dust within my shadow lie,
While the soul flying from its first found home
Comes to me with the dreams it had of me."

XXX

I lean back. I am ripe for dreams to-day;
For who that rests beneath a sky like this
Could shirk their soft existence, and so miss
Communings that etherealise the clay?
Rome is her own wide grave, and there can be
No aftermath for her. The wise and good—
Her foster children—claim'd it as they stood.
Through the spent avalanche of the years I see
The light of each great soul, and, dreaming on,
What Rome was sinks, as if to make a base
To the grand structure of the mind which God

Seals as a symbol of Himself alone;
I enter; though I cannot see His face
I know that I am near His pure abode.

XXXI

Roma! Roma! Roma! Thus, my lips
Took the soft language of the glowing skies
Of Italy. A stranger with dim eyes
Takes leave of thee, and like a shadow slips
From thy fair presence. With me I had brought
Dreams of my boyhood, and I take away
Others of sadder colour, as one may
When leaving the still room wherein our thought
Is with the sainted dead. But as I go
I feel that ever after in my breast
What Rome has been, and is, will take its rest,
And be a picture in me, with the glow
Of sunset over it. Her mighty great
Are with her to the end, above her fate.

XXXII

The ruins of years—nay, Time himself—are here;
I sit within them; but the brooding heart
Wanders to Florence, to become a part
Of one, by whom, as we walk with our peer,
Sorrow went forth, nor left him till he died—
Dante, upon whose cheek the grime of hell
Seems half-wash'd off by the hot tears that fell
At sight of those that wail'd on either side.
He stood in heaven with that spot, but still
The effluence from the celestial glow
Of her who led him, made him feel the ill
He left behind on earth. So stern yet meek
He went, not looking up, but bent his brow,
Conscious of all the stains upon his cheek.

XXXIII

Florence! they cried, and as they spoke, I stood,
And said—the quick tears filling up my eyes—

Dante's lost city, which, with life-long sighs,
He yearn'd for, and from which the sullen brood
Of factions drove him. Had he found this home,
One marvel less had been in books, and we
Had seen no vision of the world to be,
Or known how far thought can be made to roam.
Dante's lost city! In these words we feel
That lone worn spirit of his break forth in sighs,
And all our own half-smitten, till we reel,
Seeing those eyes that seem so sunk and dull,
By looking on the gnawing of the skull,
Or blinded by the light of Paradise.

XXXIV

Infinite sorrow, like a martyr's crown,
Rests upon Dante. And those stern sad eyes
Can hide it not, though ever looking down,
While those of Beatrice pierce the seventh skies.
Dost thou remember how we stood, and kept
Our gaze upon the picture where the two
Were thus seen? She so pure and sweet to view:
He earthy, though within the heavens. I wept,
Touch'd with the spirit of his grief, which spoke
To mine, until when from my trance I woke
I heard thee say—"In these two are express'd
The higher and the lower nature, which,
Being within us, we are claim'd by each,
Like the two spirits in Faust's weary breast."

XXXV

The rapt diviner poets struggle still,
Like angels with one wing, to reach their heaven,
Though it may be with dust-soil'd pinion, till
Death pities, and the other wing is given.
This earth is not for them, and when they come
They stand as strangers, till, at last, they speak
Their mission in keen words, through which we hear
The low deep yearning to regain their home,
That, though they stand on earth, is ever near,
Till the light fades upon their brow and check;
Then Heaven takes back its own that was so sweet.
In this thought I can lie in Italy,

And roll aside part of the sky, and see
Beatrice with Dante at her feet.

XXXVI

In England now! and yet the Rome I left
Follows me like a shadow. I can still
Limn forth those ruins, which men's hands and skill
Made for the ages. But the Goth hath cleft
His ruthless way, and Time has followed him.
The Forum, Colosseum, Capitol,
The palace of the Cæsars dark and dim,
The Circus and the Pantheon, the soul
Of what Rome was, her temples—all is dead
But that which was of Heaven; the far thought
Of poet, sage, historian, still have part
In all the present; Sculpture bows her head,
And full-eyed Painting, with her glorious art,
Puts down her footstep, hallowing all the spot.

XXXVII

To-morrow I will be with thee, and break
Upon thy silence, and thy treasured books.
In fancy I can see thy eager looks
And hear thy sudden questions, as we take
Our evening walk adown the little street.
How did I feel when in the evening hour
I stood within the Forum, with the power
Of Cicero upon me? Did my feet
Half shrink to touch the ground where the abodes
Of men bad been who were fit mates for gods?
And last—What have you brought me? For I crave
Some souvenir of fallen Rome, and I,
Knowing thy early warship will reply—
A wither'd violet from Keats's grave.

AGNES DIED

A pure sweet one that came but for a while,
As flowers come, and then went back to heaven,
To whom, as light unites in light, was given

The gentle purpose, and the tender smile
Of all fair things; who, dying, left behind
The gracious memory of all her ways,
The quiet raptures of melodious days,
The folded blossom of her child-like mind.

And I who still remain can feel the band
Of her fair life on mine, as from the skies
We feel the sunshine which we walk among,
Nay, more; if I could touch the spirit land,
To look for Agnes in the sinless throng,
I know I still should know her from her eyes.

I KNOW not how it is, but all the past
Is with me, speaking of its early things,
As old men like to talk about their youth.
And in its voice a clearer, sweeter chord
Is heard, and I, half in a waking dream,
Musing upon the music, think a while
Like one who on a sudden sees two paths
Before him, and, uncertain which to take,
Halts for a moment till his eye alights
On some familiar mark or shape of hill
Seen years before, and straightway goes his way;
So, thinking on that voice, a gracious time
Comes back, and in its light I stand, and say,
A touch of sorrow in my whisper, "Strange
That there should be so much to move my soul
In words so plain and simple—Agnes died."

But let me trace a pathway through the years,
Whose tombs are pillars bearing up the past,
And lay my hand upon that time when she
Knew not the shadow creeping on her cheek,
Dulling its roses, but in happy strength
Met the sweet brow of every day that brought
Glad youth and all its fairy world to her.
The first of our acquaintance sprung from where
Most human friendships spring—the school, and we,
Half shy and strange at first, broke up the ground
With words of little use to older heads,
And questions, such as owe their birth to all
The inventive gift of children free to choose
What their quick fancy thinks is best; and now
You may be looking for a long account
Of wandering slowly home in afternoons,
Amid the loyal waste of summer light;

Of holidays in which we tasted heaven;
Of the long looking forward to that time
When six weeks made us like the kings and queens
In olden stories which when brought to mind
Bring back the child into our heart once more,
And all again is sunshine.   But, alas,
I lack the fitting dress of words—not thought—
For, looking back, the glory of that time
Rises like light upon the dark, and makes
A halo round it, beautiful and bright,
As if we saw the sun through our own tears.

So we grew up, and with the kindly years
Our friendship grew the stronger, and I watch'd
With a boy lover's eye the opening bud
Of her sweet spirit; saw its infant germ
Expand beneath the breathing of the years,
Touch the soft outline of her gentle form,
And tint the cheek with colour like the rose
When first it breaks its little cell of green;
So I, who made her centre of my thought,
Became her worshipper; for when we know
The purity of that to which we bow
We grow sincere indeed.   And she was all
That one might picture Eve to be when in
The slumber of her Paradise she woke,
And found herself within the clasp of flowers.

What wonder, then, if Agnes, yet a child,
Was to me all I wish'd for, that my life
Took half its being from the warmth of hers;
That all my motions were as if her eyes
Kept watch upon me; that my sleep became
The silent picture of the day, and set
The sweet rehearsal of my waking thoughts
Before me in the fairy hue of dreams;
That her sweet voice made all my pulses thrill,
While the light touch of her ethereal hand
Made the heart quicken, as beneath the shock
Of strangely started fears or open wrong.
O! love like this is worth ten years of all
The staider bearing of a sober manhood.
And if, perchance, we smile at all the warmth
Of boyish passion in those early days,
It reaches further than the lips, and in
The heart we feel the sadness living on,
Crown'd with the vain regret, the broken light
Of an existence only to be seen

Lighting some distant peak within the heart.
So I in Agnes found another life,
And felt the wonder of another land,
As if an angel had come down from heaven
To fill me with a little of his joy.
But did her eyes find out this love of mine,
And catch the worship which I wrapp'd her in?
This was the question which I ask'd myself,
But found no fitting answer to reply;
For she partook so much of simple things,
And had such purity of thought and speech,
That if a thought of love had wing'd its flight
Across the open spaces of her heart,
It would have lost itself at once within
The fair fresh foliage of its innocent depths,
As when a bird will fly across a vale
And sink from sight amid a wealth of leaves.
Thus thought I, as the happy days flew on,
Flinging their sweetest light on me, until
A shadow fell upon my heart, and struck
The blossoms I had form'd, as when a hand
Strikes all unwittingly a feeble rose,
Whose leaves—full spent and ripe—fling down at once
Their rosy graces on the heedless ground.
For Agnes changed, and yet no change I knew,
But still it was a change, for which no name
Grew on the lip; a fear, a little hint,
The shadow of a shadow, yet afar,
The unseen touch of some sweet angel's hand,
That none could see but Death—who, passing by,
Stood for a moment ere he went away
And left his smile to mingle with her own.
But let me try to paint that one sweet day
We spent within the woods, before her strength
Grew a soft traitor, and confined her steps
To the hushed precincts of her sacred room.

The sun was bright that day, and all the sky
Glimmer'd like magic with its sunniest light,
As if it knew that I, in later times,
Would look back on that fading light, and sigh,
And sadden at that splendour sunk in death.
We took our way along a path which kept
Our footsteps by a lake, wherein was seen
A little island dripping to the edge
With golden lilies, double in their bloom;
When some, more amorous than the rest, leant o'er
And nodded to their shadows seen below.

The coot came forth at times to show the speck
Of white upon his wings, then swept away
Behind the twisted roots.   The silent heron,
Amid the tiny pillars of the reed,
Kept eager watch, nor stirr'd upon his post,
But stood a feather'd patience waiting prey;
While in the woods the birds, as if ashamed
Of all their silence through the silent night,
Gave forth in concert one great gush of song,
That flooded all things, till the very leaves
Flutter'd to find a voice to vent their joy.
We heard the piping of the amorous thrush—
The bird that sings with all his soul in heaven—
The mellow blackbird, and the pert redbreast,
Whose song was bolder than his own bright eye;
While fainter notes of lesser choristers
Came in like semitones to swell the whole;
While over all, to crown this one great song,
The lark—the grey Apollo of his race,
The feather'd Pan, the spirit clad in song—
High up, and in the very sight of heaven,
Pour'd downward with the brightness of the smiles
Of angels all his spirit, leaving doubts
Whether his song belong'd to God or us.
And there we sat within the woods, and saw
The lake between the trees, and now and then
The gentle shadow of a cloud above
Passing along its bosom, as a thought
Across the calmness of a poet's brow.
And all around the lilies grew, and on
The bank beside us, rearing its sweet head,
The azure fairy of the woodland grass,
That has a spot of heaven for its eye,
The violet nestled, while, close by its side,
The primrose, yellow star of earth's green sky,
Peep'd up in quick surprise, and, further on,
An orchis, like the fiery orb of Mars,
Rose up with purple mouth agape to catch
All murmurs and all scents that came its way.

So in this Paradise we sat, until
We broke the silence with soft speech, to fit
The purer thought which, at the golden touch
Of the pure things beside us, grew within,
Blowing to instant blossom.   Then our talk
Took simple bounds, and, with a fond delight,
We touch'd on all the heart will think, when youth
Ranges throughout its chambers; like to one

Who dares the sanctity of some fair room,
And finds in every corner fresh delight.
But I was bound by one great spell which she
Knew nothing of. I could not speak my love,
Nor could she see it, though in that sweet guise
In which we hide it only to be seen.

And so the converse sped—now quick at times,
Now slow, and then an interval in which
We went through all the paths of spoken thought,
Making the pleasure double by retouching
In silence the past interchange of words.
We felt the welcome of the summer day,
We heard its music rising everywhere;
Yet strange that all our thoughts should slip away
And strike a chord that beat not unison
With all this joy; for from our dreams and smiles
We shrunk, and, with a shadow in our eyes,
We struck upon the cypress'd edge of death.
Then solemn grew our converse, and she spoke
In low, sweet whispers, which to me were spells
Of deeper quiet, as she strove to make
A land wherein a great world moves like ours
Distinct and clear to all the grosser eye;
And simple as herself she painted heaven.
She knew not, as she spoke, how all my heart
Follow'd her words, and hung upon their tones
Helpless, and with no wish to change the task,
But catch the eloquence of what she spoke,
For truth lives nowhere but in simple words.

I hear her voice again this very hour
Clear and distinct, as if the death it wore
Made it the clearer, even as two friends,
Apart from each, but with a lake between,
Will keep up converse, losing not a word,
Because the faithful waters lie between.
So the pure essence of an unseen sweetness,
Breathing out odours from the land of death,
Speaks to me, and my spirit at each word
Wafted from lips that have no human breath,
Sighs like green leaves beneath the summer rain
When all the clouds are weeping tears of joy.

But let me to the end, nor lengthen out
This memory only for myself, for dreams
Bring to the dreamers only pain or joy,
In two weeks after, all I held as sweet

And pure of Agnes was within the grave.
For since time found a being comes this truth,
The sweetest heart within the sweetest breast
Beats not a tune to gain the ear of Death.
So Agnes died, as flowers will die when frost
Falls, ere the sun is up, upon their bloom;
Or when some curious hand will open up
The undeveloped bud, that by its hue
The eye may picture forth the perfect flower,
And shape a pleasure for the coming years.
Thus into the great garden of this life
Came Death, and, lighting with an eager eye
Upon the bud I thought would bloom for me,
He prest aside the leaves that hid as yet
The glorious promise of a glorious flower,
Letting its unripe fragrance sink and die
Upon the bosom of the careless air,
And so despoil'd it; leaving unto me
The scatter'd leaves to gather up at will.
So Agnes went away, when all her life
Stood like a prophet, mixing in its cup
Rare hopes, and novel tasks, and gentle dreams,
That took their colour from her own pure heart;
And just as she had raised it to her lips
To touch the golden nectar, lo! it fell
In rainbow pieces at her stricken feet;
And from the fragments lying now in dust,
As jewels glimmer through the barren sand,
Have I shaped out this sacred memory
Of her who rose upon my young pure life
First planet there, as in the midnight sky
A meteor lingers till it grasps the sight,
Then shooting paler light across the heaven,
Fades, as a smile might from an angel's lips,
Behind the silver fretwork of the stars.

BLOOD ON THE WHEEL

"Bless her dear little heart!" said my mate, and he pointed out to me,
Fifty yards to the right, in the darkness, a light burning steady and clear.
"That's her signal in answer to me, when I whistle, to let me see
She is at her place by the window the time I am passing here."

I turn'd to look at the light, and I saw the tear on his cheek—
He was tender of heart, and I knew that his love was lasting and strong—
But he dash'd it off with his hand, and I did not think fit to speak,

But look'd right ahead through the dark, as we clank'd and thunder'd along.

They had been at the school, the two, and had run, like a single life,
Through the mazes of childhood up to the sweeter and firmer prime,
And often he told me, smiling, he had promised to make her his wife,
In the rambles they had for nuts in the woods in the golden autumn time.

"I must make," he would add, "that promise good in the course of a month or two;
And then, when I have her safe and sound in a nook of the busy town,
No use of us whistling then, Joe, lad, as now we incline to do,
For a wave of her hand, or an answering light as we thunder up and down."

Well, the marriage was settled at last, and I was to stand by his side,
Take a part in the happy rite, and pull from his hand the glove;
And still as we joked between ourselves, he would say, in his manly pride,
That the very ring of the engine-wheels had something in them of love.

At length we had just one run to make before the bridal took place,
And it happen'd to be in the night, yet merry in heart we went on;
But long ere he came to the house, he was turning each moment his face
To catch the light by the window, placed as a beacon for him alone.

"Now then, Joe," he said, with his hand on my arm, "keep a steady look-out ahead
While I whistle for the last time;" and he whistled sharply and clear;
But no light rose up at the sound; and he look'd with something like dread
On the white-wash'd walls of the cot, through the gloom looking dull, and misty, and drear.

But lo! as he turn'd to whistle again, there rose on the night a scream,
And I rush'd to the side in time to catch the flutter of something white;
Then a hitch through the engine ran like a thrill, and in haste he shut off the steam,
While we stood looking over at each with our hearts beating wild with affright.

The station was half a mile ahead, but an age seem'd to pass away
Ere we came to a stand, and my mate, as a drunken man will reel,
Rush'd on to the front with his lamp, but to bend and come back and say,
In a whisper faint with its terror—"Joe, come and look at this blood on the wheel."

Great heaven! a thought went through my heart like the sudden stab of a knife,
While the same dread thought seem'd to settle on him and palsy his heart and mind,
For he went up the line with the haste of one who is rushing to save a life,
And with the dread shadow of what was to be I follow'd closely behind.

What came next is indistinct, like the mist on the mountain side—
Gleam of lights and awestruck faces, but one thing can never grow dim:
My mate, kneeling down in his grief like a child by the side of his mangled bride,
Kill'd, with the letter still in her hand she had wish'd to send to him.

Some little token was in it, perhaps to tell of her love and her truth,

Some little love-errand to do ere the happy bridal drew nigh;
So in haste she had taken the line, but to meet, in the flush of her fair sweet youth,
The terrible death that could only be seen with a horror in heart and eye.

Speak not of human sorrow—it cannot be spoken in words;
Let us veil it as God veil'd His at the sight of His Son on the cross.
For who can reach to the height or the depth of those infinite yearning chords
Whose tones reach the very centre of heaven when swept by the fingers of loss?

She sleeps by the little ivied church in which she had bow'd to pray—
Another grave close by the side of hers, for he died of a broken heart,
Wither'd and shrunk from that awful night like the autumn leaves in decay,
And the two were together that death at first had shaken so roughly apart.

But still, when I drive through the dark, and that night comes back to my mind,
I can hear the shriek take the air, and beneath me fancy I feel
The engine shake and hitch on the rail, while a hollow voice from behind
Cries out, till I leap on the footplate, "Joe, come and look at this blood on the wheel!"

CHATEAUX EN ESPAGNE

It is a pleasant thing to rhyme,
Providing it but bring you money;
But sweeter still to pass the time
In building fabrics high and sunny.
Alnaschar, ere he bent his knee
To give a climax to his lecture,
Could by no chance have mated me
At atmospheric architecture.

From early boyhood I began
To follow Vathek, and erected
A goodly pile, upon a plan
That was not with due care inspected.
I rear'd up columns rich with fret,
And all the cunning of the gilder;
But somehow, to my deep regret,
They always fell upon their builder.

I rear'd in many a forest black
Huge castles by deep moats defended;
And strode their master, mail on back,
With half-a-dozen knights attended.
We sat, like those of Branksome Hall,
In armour, just as we were able,
And drank red wine from goblets tall,

And clash'd mail'd hands across the table.

From this you cannot fail to guess
That I was with the Middle Ages,
And never was at ease unless
With stately dames and graceful pages.
But what with manhood sober'd down,
Those dreams that made me so despotic
Have burst their chrysalis, and flown,
And left me others less Quixotic.

And now, when in my building mood,
And all my whims have free expansion,
I shape within a sober wood
An old discolour'd Gothic mansion.
You scarce can see it for the trees
That kindly interlace their branches,
Through which the sunshine slips at ease,
And falls in sunny avalanches.

Around are long and shady walks,
That lead in many a quaint direction—
Fit haunts for sage who sighs and talks,
And shakes his head as in dejection;
Or some bold poet, when his thought
Was at its swiftest mood for seizing
The glowing images it sought,
And mould them into something pleasing.

Clear leaping fountains here and there
Through all the summer day are playing;
Soft winds are coming through the air,
That bring sweet incense in their straying.
And statues from the Greek are set—
Aglow with all their snowy graces—
In nooks where drooping leaves are met,
And half conceal them in their places.

But in my own sweet sanctum, where
No outer noise dare make intrusion,
You ought to pay a visit there,
And see the poet in seclusion.
The rich light falls upon the wall,
Then fades away to something fainter,
Before white marble busts, and all
The masterpieces of the painter.

Here as you enter, on your left

A Goethe stands, whose marble vision
Seems still to keep that light which cleft
Through all this life with such precision.
While on your right, with upturn'd brow,
A Schiller stands, with noble presence,
To teach one all the upward glow
Revolving round the purer essence.

Then right before me where I sit
A Milton looks across to Dante,
Whose brows contract, as loth to fit
The slender sprig of laurel scanty.
These two would always catch my eye
When looking up for inspiration,
And teach me, when the mood was high,
To mould the keen imagination.

In every nook within the room
My favourite books get sacred lodgment—
Word-webs from the brain's restless loom,
Spun out with truth and sober judgment.
A hundred spirits there repose,
Who, at my slightest will and pleasure,
As Ariel did at Prospero's,
Kneel down and offer up their treasure.

Like Southey, all my days would be
Among the dead, but that is lying;
The mighty dead, it seems to me,
Are those that only are undying.
Of course they take our death, a pain
Which we, as humankind, inherit,
And pass for ever, to remain
Swift's struldbrugs living in the spirit.

But I digress.   Not all alone
Am I within this learnèd palace,
For, as the twilight wanders on
And feels along the distant valleys,
The door creeps softly back, and then
A fairy creature growing bolder
Comes in, and, soft as falling rain,
Lays both her hands upon my shoulder

Then turning round, I see a face
Where love with rounded youth is blended,
And all the nameless winning grace,
Above my own all softly bended;

And, ere I can get time to speak,
Or smile a welcome at the meeting,
Two little lips, all coy and meek,
Against my own press rosy greeting.

Then, sitting on my knee, she slips
One arm around me, while the other
Comes down, until her finger tips
Are in my beard to plague and bother.
And still she whispers, while her look
Turns sad to see my deep abstraction—
"Come, take a rest, your last new book
Might surely give you satisfaction."

But just as I put up my hand
To bring her head a little nearer,
To kiss the lips that so command,
And tell her she is growing dearer—
Beim himmel! swift as lightning flies,
My statues, mansion, wife and fountains
Dissolve, and I—I rub my eyes,
Like Rip Van on the Kaatskill mountains.

And so, instead of all my fame,
My pictures, busts—both Greek and Roman—
A wife, a noble after—name,
Which makes its owner envy no man;
Instead of running into town
To see the last new book or picture,
Or hear some oracle full grown
Deliver philosophic stricture:

In lieu of this, a case of books,
A little room confined and narrow,
That might have sour'd the anxious looks
Of Faust, whose thoughts eat to the marrow;
A little desk, where all my brains
Get warp'd with long Parnassian creepers,
And dull'd throughout the day by trains,
Pick, shovel, hammers, rails, and sleepers.

BLIND MATTHEW

Blind Matthew, coming down the village street
With slow, sure footsteps, pauses for a while,
And in the sunlight falling soft and sweet

His features brighten to a kindly smile.

Upon his ear the sounds of toil and gain,
Clanking from wood-girt shop and smithy, steal,
And soft he whispers, "O my fellow-men,
I cannot see you, but I hear and feel."

Then smiling still he slowly steps along,
And every kindly word and friendly tone,
Like the old fragment of an early song,
Wakes thoughts that make the past again his own.

The children see him, and in merry band
Come shouting from their glad and healthy play,
"Here is blind Matthew, let us take his hand,
And see if he can guess our names to-day."

Then all around him throng, and run, and press,
And lead him to his seat beneath the tree,
Each striving to be first, for his caress,
Or gain the favour'd seat upon his knee.

And Matthew, happy in their artless prate,
Cries, as he slips into their guileless plan,
"Now she who holds my right hand is sweet Kate,
And she who holds my left is little Anne."

Then all the children leap with joyful cries,
Till one fair prattler nestling on his breast
Whispers, "Blind Matthew, tell us when your eyes
Shall have their light, and open like the rest?"

Then closer still he draws the little one,
Laying his hand upon her golden head;
Then speaks with low, soft, sweet and solemn tone,
While all the rest range round with quiet tread.

He tells how Christ, in ages long ago,
Came down to earth in human shape and name,
Walking his pilgrimage, begirt with woe,
And laying healing hands on blind and lame.

Then of blind Bartimeus, the beggar, he
Who by the wayside sat, and cried in awe,
Jesus, thou Son of David, look on me;"
And Jesus look'd and touch'd him, and he saw.

"But not on earth these eyes of mine shall fill

With light," thus Matthew ends, "for in this night
I must grope on with Christ to guide me still,
And He will lead me through the grave to light.

"So when you miss old Matthew from the street,
And in the quiet of the churchyard lies
A new-made grave, to draw your timid feet,
Then will you know that Christ has touch'd my eyes."

ADA

Lying full-length upon the summer grass,
And by the murmur of a summer stream,
I heard the village bell, and turning round
To him who sat beside me with his feet
Touching the ripple of the brook, I said,
"Who sinks into the churchyard rest to-day?"
Then he, half lifting up his earnest face,
Paused for a little while, and then replied
"Ada, whose beauty was a fairy thing,
But brighter now by Death, whose pencil tints
His marks with such sweet colours."

Then he sunk
Into that dreamy reverie which shuts
All thought from out its vision, and so thinks,
And thinks, and thinks, and yet thinks naught at all;
But I, half-answer'd, could but ill abide
His silentness, and so I question'd still:
"But who is Ada? you have never said;
And there you dream, and think, and all the while
The tolling of the bell within my ear,
And yet I know not unto whom it offers
Such sweet and stirless rest."

Then starting up
From all his fit of mute philosophy
He said, "Why, surely you have not forgot
Ada, who flash'd upon you like a star
Three months ago, when you were in the woods.
At your old rambles, and she knew it not,
But pass'd you in her beauty by, and you
Fell half in love with her and writ a song?"

Then all at once came, like remember'd dreams,
The solitude around the woodland walk,

And all the fringing of the idle rhyme
(Now something better by the help of Death),
Which I had made in haste, and sung to him
A half-hour after. "Now, what better time
Than this," I cried, "to sing that song again,
When she is passing from all mortal view
Into the shady quietness." And he,
Catching the broader finish of the plan,
Said, "Let the song be sung, but make a pause
Between each stanza, that the bell may chime
Its echoes at the finish of each verse,
And let your poet's fancy shape the words."
So, with the humming idyll of the brook
As an accompaniment I sang the song:

Ada came down by the path in the wood,
In the flush and the warmth of the day,
And the spirits that live in the solitude
(For there be such they say)
Came out from their haunts by tree and brook,
And wherever sunbeams play,
To gaze, as she pass'd like a bud on the lake—
A sweet Diana of earthly make—
In the clasp of the amorous day.

I ceased, and the sad bell took up the pause,
And sang an answer to its solemn chime:

Ada walks no earthly path,
Other things are hers this hour;
She has all an angel hath—
Glory and celestial power;
Nought may look on her but eyes
Purged from aught of mortal sight,
As she walks in balmy light
In the halls of Paradise.
So the dust may shrink, but she
Through the years, in the spheres,
Is one great type of immortality.

So sang the bell, and when its echo died
I took my part in turn, and sang again:

I was out in the wood when she pass'd me by,
Half-hid that she could not see,
So a woman's wish was in her eye,
And a smile that made me, I know not why,
Guess and dream that she

Was far away in the golden hope
Of the coming time, and the novel scope
Of wifehood, and the prattling bliss
Of little lips, and this, and this
Was the light and colour within her eye,
And the smile as she pass'd me by.

JENNY WI' THE AIRN TEETH

What a plague is this o' mine,
Winna steek his e'e,
Though I hap him ow'r the head
As cosie as can be.
Sleep! an' let me to my wark,
A' thae claes to airn;
Jenny wi' the airn teeth,
Come an' tak' the bairn:

Tak' him to your ain den,
Where the bowgie bides,
But first put baith your big teeth
In his wee plump sides;
Gie your auld grey pow a shake,
Rive him frae my grup—
Tak' him where nae kiss is gaun
When he waukens up.

Whatna noise is that I hear
Comin' doon the street?
Weel I ken the dump-dump
O' her beetle feet.
Mercy me, she's at the door,
Hear her lift the sneck;
Whisht! an' cuddle mammy noo
Closer roun' the neck.

Jenny wi' the airn teeth,
The bairn has aff his claes,
Sleepin' safe an' soun', I think—
Dinna touch his taes;
Sleepin' weans are no for you;
Ye may turn about
An' tak' awa' wee Tam next door—
I hear him screichin' oot.

Dump, dump, awa' she gangs

Back the road she cam';
I hear her at the ither door,
Speirin' after Tam.
He's a crabbit, greetin' thing,
The warst in a' the toon;
Little like my ain wee wean—
Losh, he's sleepin' soun'.

Mithers hae an awfu' wark
Wi' their bairns at nicht—
Chappin' on the chair wi' tangs
To gi'e the rogues a fricht.
Aulder weans are fley'd wi' less,
Weel aneuch we ken—
Bigger bowgies, bigger Jennies,
Frichten muckle men.

JAMIE'S WEE CHAIR

The snawdrap was oot, and the primrose was seen
In the cleuch, while the side o' the burnie was green;
The mavis was heard singin' sweet in the wud,
While a safter licht fell frae the edge o' the clud;
The whaups an' the peaseweeps skirl'd lood on the hill,
When the pride o' the hoose, oor wee Jamie, fell ill;
But lang ere that snawdrap had wither'd an' gane,
A wee grave was a' we had left o' oor wean.

'Twas an unco sair trial for baith John an' me,
For the bairnie was just the tae licht o' my e'e.
As for him, he scarce ken'd what he whiles wud be at,
Wi' his wee Jamie this and his wee Jamie that;
But that nicht when Death cam' in white licht owre his broo,
He said, takin' my han', "Jean, that's owre wi' us noo;"
Then he sat down an' grat, cryin', half in despair,
"We hae naebody noo to fill Jamie's wee chair."

I bore up mysel', wi' the tear on my cheek,
An' the thochts in my heart that I couldna weel speak,
An' aften I took a step ben to the room
To kiss the wee lips that still keepit their bloom;
But at last, when the day cam' to tak' him away,
An' the last o' the fouk was seen climbin' the brae,
I cam' in frae the door, an' I grat lang an' sair,
Wi' my heid on the airm o' my Jamie's wee chair.

O, the bliss o' warm tears when the sair heart is fu',
Fa'in' saft on oor grief like kind Heaven's ain dew,
Till, as rain lowns the win', so the sorrow that fain
Wad rise up against God settles calmly again;
An', as saft, siller cluds an' the wide, happy sky
Turn the brichter and bluer when storms hae gaen by,
Sae the gloom roun' my life lichten'd up everywhere
As I rase an' took ben my deid Jamie's wee chair.

Then I took doon the plaicks frae the shelf on the wa',
The whussle, the peerie, the pony, an' ba',
Put them safe in the drawer; an', when I had dune,
The door saftly open'd, an' John steppit in.
He stood just awee, then began to look roun',
But stoppit on seein' the plaicks a' ta'en doon;
Then he spier'd, his voice shakin' wi' grief mair an' mair,
"Jean, where hae ye puttin oor Jamie's wee chair?"

I rase, as he spoke, frae the cheerless fire en',
Gaed into the room, brocht the chair quately ben,
Put it into its place, never liftin' an e'e,
But sat doon, while John drew himsel' nearer to me;
Then I fan' his braid ban' tak' a grup o' my ain,
As he said, "Jean, it's a' for the sake o' the wean,
For ye ken weel aneuch that the bairn last sat there,
So atween us this forenicht we'll keep his wee chair."

We drew near the hearth, the tears fillin' oor een
As we sat han'-in-han' wi' the wee chair atween;
An' aye as we thocht on a bricht lauchin' face,
An' a curly bit heid noo nae mair in its place,
We turn'd, as if a' oor sair loss was a name,
An' wee Jamie wad juist be aside us the same.
O, it tak's unco schulin', an' God's help an' care,
To mak' mithers believe in an empty wee chair.

We sat, while the hills creepit close in the nicht;
But the stars, lookin' doon, kent that a' wasna richt,
For they whisper'd to me o' a joy yet in store,
An' a something abune them I ne'er had afore.
I turn'd roun' to John, laid my ban' on his knee,
As I tell 't what the stars keepit sayin' to me;
Then we kneel'd doon, oor hearts risin' up in a prayer,
As oor heids met aboon oor deid Jamie's wee chair.

Years hae gaen by since thaun, but still warm in oor heart
What the stars said has aye been fulfillin' its pairt;
An' we see noo that a' was intended for guid,

Though God's han' at the time by oor sorrow was hid;
But as rainbows are brichter against a black sky,
So God's meanin's grow clear when His shadow gangs by;
An' in a' the bit trials that fa' to oor share,
We aye keep atween us oor Jamie's wee chair.

A WALK TO PAMPHY LINNS

The following poem was the result of a visit which I, along with three others, paid to Pamphy linns, a romantic spot lying hidden in a wood which stretches along the Barr Moor in the neighbourhood of Sanquhar. I have availed myself of a poetical license, and described the linns as swollen by rains, and foaming down the waterfall which forms the pièce de resistance of the place. The friends who accompanied me will pardon me where I have deviated from fact to fiction, especially my young Edinburgh friend whom I have bored in the text. The poem is warmly dedicated to the three.

We took a walk to Pamphy linns—
Three other friends and I,
Glad-hearted as when day begins
With summer in the sky.

Our talk was edged with homely wit,
The banter flew apace,
And ever at a happy hit
The laughter clad our face.

But we were used to each, and knew
The harmless fence of tongue;
So quip and jest rose up and flew
And prick'd, but never stung.

The lark was far above our head,
The daisy at our feet,
The heather show'd a coming red
Of tiny blossom sweet.

The sheep turn'd round to see us pass,
The milky snow-white lambs
Gamboll'd and sniff'd the growing grass,
Or nestled by their dams.

The pure air brought the far hills near,
Their furrows came to sight;
And here and there a stream grew clear,
And smiled in the sunlight.

"O, friend of mine, who late," I said,

"Has left the streets of men,
Let all this quiet overhead
Bring back thine own again.

Look how the Earth puts forth her pride
And blooms around, to draw
Thy soul out till it toss aside
The phrases of the law.

For what are musty words to this—
Your writs and pros and cons—
When Nature, full of summer bliss,
Her summer vesture dons?

So, Faust-like, own her quiet power,
And let her have her will,
And let thy fingers clasp a flower,
Instead of inky quill."

Our path lay through the sunny fields,
In gentle ups and downs;
Dear heart! I thought, but nature yields
A bliss unmatch'd in towns.

At length we reach'd a shepherd's cot,
That sat between two woods—
Fit home for all the stirless thought
That, dove-like, sits and broods.

I knew the shepherd; for a space
We rested by his hearth,
And saw the moorland on his face,
And in his honest mirth.

O! blessings on a hillside life
That trammels not the heart,
But in its gentle pleasures rife
Stands with its back to art.

How far above the studied speech
Of empty polish'd sound,
That glides within a proper reach,
Where rule has set the bound.

And blessings on the girl who stood
In better garb than silk,
And proffer'd to us, shy of mood,
A glass of cooling milk.

Her cheek was soft with health's fair tint,
And in her drooping eye
Sweet thoughts came up that fain would hint
That maidenhood was nigh.

Her brow was open, frank, and free,
Half-hid by wealth of tress—
A very Wordsworth's girl was she
For woodland simpleness.

So, Janet, half-way through thy teens,
And all the world to learn,
Lean to thine own sweet heart, as leans
From moss-clad rock the fern:

And hear the wish that springs from mine
Before I pass away—
Keep thou that simple life of thine,
Take to the town who may.

We reach'd a belt of wood at last,
And with a lusty cheer
I cried, "Now all our toil is past,
For Pamphy linns are here."

We took the shaded path that led
To the turf clad foot-bridge,
Then struck into the streamlet's bed,
And held along its edge.

We reach'd the falls, and, looking round,
On either side were trees,
And at our feet the hurrying sound
Of water ill at ease.

Huge rocks with moss half-cover'd dipt
Or in the stream reclined,
As if they once had partly stript
To bathe, but changed their mind.

O'er these the water foam'd and splash'd
In many a whirl and turn,
Or from moss'd outlets peep'd and dash'd
To kiss a wander'd fern.

We clomb the highest peak of rock,
And, halting there to breathe,

Heard with continual splash and shock
The water run beneath.

Then, rising, down the fretted steep
To reach the base below
We struggled, careful heed to keep,
As Alpine hunters go.

We reach'd the foot, and found a rest
Beneath the trees' sweet shade,
Where Nature for her woodland guest
A flower-deck'd seat had made.

From there we watch'd the falls above,
The rocks half-worn and gray,
That still, like shapeless Sphinxes, strove
To tear their veils of spray.

A dreamy, cooling murmur went,
Like winds when spring is near,
Through all the trees, that stood intent,
And prick'd their leaves to hear.

I leant back in a shady place,
Where sunlight could not gleam:
If poets are a dreaming race,
Then here they well might dream.

But "Further down," was still the cry—
"Down to the seat," they said;
"There let another hour go by—
The hanging rocks o'erhead."

So there we went, and with our knives
We roughly carved our names,
As some carve out their shorten'd lives
With vacillating aims.

And as I carved, a primrose bright
Look'd on with wondrous eye,
As if for ever in its sight
A troop of fays pass'd by.

Upon the rocks, from German rhyme,
I writ two lines to say—
"O, happy time of love's young prime,
Would it could last alway?" [1.]

But ere we turn'd our path to trace,
I cried, "Farewell, thou stream!
If poets are a dreaming race,
Then here they well might dream."

So through the woods we went, but still
What German Schiller sung
Came ever up against my will,
And somewhat lightly stung.

O, happy time when love is sweet,
And life takes little heed,
But rolls a rainbow at our feet,
Would it could last indeed!

And every flower in shaded nook,
Speedwell and violet,
Cried, with a wonder in their look—
So big, and dreaming yet?

Then out at last into the fields,
Tinged with the daisy's dyes;
Dear heart! I said, but Nature yields
A bliss the town denies;

For here she dwells, and keeps apart
From all the busy street,
Still talking with her own rich heart,
Whose lightest thought is sweet.

And yet, as when in dreams we see
A city built of air,
So rose a vision unto me
That sent my thoughts elsewhere.

Edina too is fair, I said,
And took my young friend's arm,
For there the magic past hath shed
An ever-growing charm.

Twice have I trod its streets, and heard
In fancy all the while
Legends in hints and whisper'd word
From narrow street and pile.

But still the eye from every quest
Would stop, to wander on
To those gray rocks that had for crest

The lordly pile of stone.

Up, up it tower'd, as if in rage
The modern, change to view;
Like Carlyle, from the middle age,
With brow knit at the new.

I, too, have touch'd Queen Mary's robe,
With well-shaped Darnley nigh;
Have heard the murder'd Rizzio sob
With blood-choked, helpless cry.

While through this war of uncheck'd will,
Its battles, broils, and shocks,
A stirring voice was speaking still—
The voice of fearless Knox.

God! when upon his grave I stood—
Now daily trod by feet—
His soul went flashing through my blood
In mighty waves of heat.

For great, good men can never die,
Howbeit the ages roll;
But still unseen are ever nigh,
To strengthen soul by soul.

But past is all that reign of force,
Its deeds of blood and pain,
Gone as a river dries its source,
Never to fill again.

For lo! to hide each bloody spot
A nobler comes behind;
The curbless sway of growing thought,
The dynasty of mind:

Which changes, and hath changed the earth,
As gods the sculptor's stone;
A universal Protean birth,
Whose fiat thunders on.

There, too, beneath the statued dome
He sits, the Scott we claim;
Fit Mahomet for those who come
As pilgrims of his fame.

Light was his task, some cry, but he,

He changed the novel's bent;
And with its Gothic tracery
A chaster purpose blent.

I pass those mighty ones, who then
Were ever in my sight—
Strong kings who struggled with the pen
To widen human right.

Yes!   She is wondrous fair, and sweet
This summer day would be
If I could lie on Arthur's Seat,
And my schoolmate with me.

For still her magic power prevails.
And still my thoughts take wing
To her, the city of the tales,
Without its roving king.

But shame on me that I should prate
Of all that city's grace
And beauty in such quiet state
Around my own sweet place.

For look! three miles adown the vale
Sanquhar lies in gray light;
And further on, time-struck and frail,
The castle lifts its height.

Bones of the iron age, it stands,
And, as to madness grown,
Flings down each year, from powerless hands,
A crutch of scatter'd stone.

And right before us, near yet far,
Furrow'd with winter rills,
That dry in summer like some scar;
Stretch out the Todholes hills.

And speck-like at their base is seen
The cot of shepherd Dryfe—
True soul of honest heart and mien,
And simple mountain life.

But here is Killo bridge, and there
Nestles old Killoside;
My blessings on the homely pair
Who 'neath its roof abide.

And right in line that puff of smoke
That every moment comes,
Is Bankhead, where, in ceaseless yoke,
The engine clanks and hums.

A little further on we pace,
Then through a field again,
And all at once, before our face,
Kirkconnel full and plain.

I see the churchyard and the church,
The gravestones standing by;
You need not through our Scotland search
For sweeter place to lie.

And further up I catch the gleam
Upon the pastor's pool;
The manse above, still as a dream,
Stands in the shadows cool.

But there, from schoolhouse to the mill,
Our hamlet stretches out;
Without one stir it slumbers still,
Save when the schoolboys shout.

And now we cross the new foot-bridge,
That spans the Nith below,
Nor loiter to lean o'er the edge
To watch the water flow;

But hasten up the narrow road
To reach the old stone seat
Beside the door, there rest and nod
To friends across the street.

1.
*"O, das sie ewig grünen bliebe,
Die schöne Zeit der jungen Liebe."*
—Das Lied von der Glocke.

CUDDLE DOON

The bairnies cuddle doon at nicht,
Wi' muckle faucht an' din;
O, try and sleep, ye waukrife rogues,

Your faither's comin' in.
They never heed a word I speak;
I try to gie a froon,
But aye I hap them up, an' cry,
"O, bairnies, cuddle doon."

Wee Jamie wi' the curly heid—
He aye sleeps next the wa',
Bangs up an' cries, "I want a piece"—
The rascal starts them a'.
I rin an' and fetch them pieces, drinks,
They stop awee the soun',
Then draw the blankets up an' cry,
"Noo, weanies, cuddle doon."

But ere five minutes gang, wee Rab
Cries oot, frae 'neath the claes,
"Mither, mak' Tam gie ower at ance,
He's kittlin' wi' his taes."
The mischief's in that Tam for tricks,
He'd bother half the toon;
But aye I hap them up an' cry,
"O, bairnies, cuddle doon."

At length they hear their faither's fit,
An', as he steeks the door,
They turn their faces to the wa',
While Tam pretends to snore.
"Hae a' the weans been gude?" he asks,
As he pits aff his shoon.
"The bairnies, John, are in their beds,
An' lang since cuddled doon."

An' just afore we bed oorsel's,
We look at oor wee lambs;
Tam has his airm roun' wee Rab's neck,
An' Rab his airm roun' Tam's.
I lift wee Jamie up the bed,
An' as I straik each croon,
I whisper, till my heart fills up,
"O, bairnies, cuddle doon."

The bairnies cuddle doon at nicht
Wi' mirth that's dear to me;
But sune the big warl's cark an' care
Will quaten doon their glee.
Yet, come what will to ilka ane,
May He who sits aboon

Aye whisper, though their pows be bauld,
"O, bairnies, cuddle doon."

ALEXIS

A passing glimpse into the life of one
Who went apart—a dreamer of fair dreams,
That fell upon his heart and made sweet spots,
As when the summer beams slip through the leaves
And pitch their camps of light upon the grass.
He went apart, for he had still within
The fair rich company of noble things,
And all that converse which belongs to youth
When hope is high and wears its fullest flower;
But he will pass, as footprints pass away,
Beneath the tread of all the hungry years
Who will not wait a moment on a name;
And with him too shall pass the many dreams
That bent their bow above his life, and drew
The heavens nearer—these will fade, and he
Will shroud himself within the past, nor leave
A light to break or line to mar that sky
Which bends a common shadow over all.
So be it. And that little space wherein
We took our daily dower of life, may grow
A ranker growth of grass or trailing weed,
Or harden with the tread of stranger feet.
What boots it, if the common grey comes down
To shade the life we led, if all the years
That lead the future onward, lift the thread
Of that fair purpose which ran through his life,
And wind it into that great cord which draws
The rough world onward to the good to be.

Alexis grew apace, and through his youth
Ran dreams and splendours, as a summer bow
Lighting upon two hills uprears its arch
Against the clouds, and all the space below
Lies warm within its shadow: So his life,
Beneath such dreams, took golden hues of light,
And beat in wonder. He was yet a child,
Standing upon the flower-grown edge of life,
Yearning for manhood, which was seen afar,
Half-veil'd 'd in shadow. Eager looks he cast
Before him to that wonder-land which sent
Sweet echoes onward, that, to his rapt ear,

Were perfect music.   To his soul within,
Expanding like a bud, these sounds became
Sure guides, that led his glowing thoughts away
To sunny regions, where the Beautiful,
Armida-like, sat canopied with roofs
Of dazzling golden fretwork.   Life to him
Was the pure surface of a glossy shell,
Seen with the eye, but felt with no rough touch.
He knew not mankind, for the gift that looks
Beneath, and shapes from word and look the key
To open beings, was not his.   He stood
A dreamer in the land of dreams, nor felt
The world jar with their action, but like one
Who feels himself drawn into some delight
And cannot turn, he went, and all the way
He had the unseen company of song,
Which, like low breathings coming from the sea,
Touch'd him to a new being, and he smiled
To think the gods had, in their idle moods,
Leant from their windless halls to touch his lips
With consecrating fire and make him sing—
A working priest of song amid his kind.
And with this thought there came to open up
His life a vision of high fame, as in the night
When the swift lightning runs a fiery track
To earth, and all the night grows white with fear:
So in Alexis rose the sudden hope
Of what might be when all this office fill'd
With the pure reaching forward of the thought
Which makes the poet; energies which strive,
Like some impulsive touch of God's, to shape
A higher life, which he forecasts himself,
And works out as he sings, still looking back
To see if any follow.   Thus in him
There was continual bud and bloom, as in
A wood that slopes to catch the first of spring,
When unseen angels open up the flowers,
And bid them turn their clear wet eyes to God.
Fancies were his which like strong sunlight made
Within his heart the prints of joy and love,
As angels' footsteps print the floor of heaven.
So he grew up, and everywhere he found
A wealth of friends, who smiling seem'd to him
The early reflex of those times when truth
Was uppermost—the strength and soul of speech.
He bent himself to all their wish, he found
A pleasure in forestalling purpose, took
Words as a pledge for the fair truth, and smiled

To see the earth roll back to all its plan.
"Then fell across his path a brighter beam,
From which his heart drank sweeter melody,
As when a sunbeam falls across a brook,
And gives a lighter music to its sound.
And she, the maiden who upon his life
Came like a wave of sunshine, as it slips
Along a field rich with the look of May,
Was fair and beautiful, and her sweet eyes
Look'd like a spirit's but half an hour in heaven.
What rapture was within him when he saw
This maiden rising up through all his dreams
To crown the inmost thoughts within his soul.
What worship shook his heart, when all the earth
Rose up, like some great organ, in whose tone
He heard the prelude to his life—we know
But cannot utter; for our deepest thoughts
Are known but to ourselves, and will not take
The garb of words.   This much we know, that she
Glided throughout his life in light and love,
As down the Ganges floats the steady light
Of one frail lamp, still telling those who watch
Far off upon the bank that all is well.
He now was in the higher bounds, and saw
The early meaning of the glorious earth
Unveil itself, and in his soul there stirr'd
A sweet unrest, that was so sweet to him;
He wish'd no other for his paradise.
This was the golden summer of his life;
The mirror of his being, in whose light
He saw the very gods pass on with smiles
And music, leaving in their odorous tracks
The incense of Olympus.   What to him
Was all the daily life of living men,
The custom and the course of earthly things?
He saw them not, for like the flower that turns
Its blossoms to the sun it follows still,
So all the thoughts and visions of the soul
Turn'd to that maiden, who for ever stood
Before him, the divinest of all things
That God hath sent into this world of ours.

We pause before we touch the other life,
To dream again the dreams Alexis dreamt;
For life moves on in change, but still the heart
Turns to the softer as the purest, best.
And thus at times our own will muse, and think
Upon Alexis, and his early dreams

So purely fashion'd; and the new-found song
That in his bosom leapt, as when a stream
Slips down a few feet into foam, and makes
A lulling music through the day and night.
This was a golden season in his life
When all the chords of being, beat as one,
And hope and love their fingers touching, each
Made melody from which sweet thoughts uprose
To fall in light upon his heart, as, when
Far off where earth and heaven seem to meet
Patches of sunlight, God's own gardening, fall
In slips of sliding glory on the hills.

He stood blindfolded with his dreams, until
The rude fact coming, with unsparing hand,
Snatch'd at the bandage which, unloosen'd, fell,
And left him face to face with sterner life.
Oh! the harsh truth that must be learn'd with tears
By those who stand a step within the pale
Of life's strange mysteries. As a towering tree,
Struck by a sudden blight, though yet in prime,
Shakes, at the sudden breathing of a wind,
Its leaves from branches shrunk and dry, so at
The shock of real life all the golden thought
Fell off, and left him with a naked heart
To front the rough world with. He stood and saw
His life-dreams lying at his very feet
Shrunk into ashes; for the one high idol
He worshipp'd, took the common form of earth,
And dwindled into a more human shape,
Laying aside divinity as one
Flings off cast clothing. All those attributes
Which he, as pilgrims deck the shrine of saints,
Had given to that maiden, fell away,
Leaving her Lamia-like to stand and prick
His dreams, until, like other human things,
They warr'd upon each other. Then he turn'd
As one may who has fought for years to reach
His life's aim but to fail, and turn away
A calm face but a bleeding heart within,
The world not heeding of it. Then his life
Fell into gaps and chasms he could not step
Or even bridge, and in him the dislike
For fellowship rose up, and made his heart
A hermit in the breast, nor gave himself
To aims and purposes that work with men,
Drawing them on and up. He made himself
An adept in tongue-fence, and stung with words

The lighter fools around him. Out of this
He made a kind of armour, under which
He found such shelter that they let him pass,
Dreading its sting. But still with this there came,
From the night-time that lay around his heart,
Voices that whisper'd higher things, and sent
A yearning through his being, felt as yet
Like idle sounds that strike upon the ear
When one lies in the shade for summer-heat,
Feeling around the edges of a dream.
Put from this sting and idle quip of tongue.
As only fit for those who deftly move
Small puppets at a village fair, he turn'd,
And made himself the guest of other minds
In other language. He was strangely stirr'd
To find the same young worship in their hearts,
The same fond idols lying in the dust,
Like broken masterpieces of dead times
When gods had temples: then the fire and heat
Of all their youth-time, sinking down to warm
The roots of manhood, growing out to flower
In high endeavour. It may be that this,
And the contagion shooting from the soul
(For all true souls stand girt in their own heat,
Warming all those who stand within it), made
Alexis find his depth, and shape his life
In other channels. In those noble ones
Who stereotype themselves in words he found
The aspirations and the high desire
To make the human take celestial shape,
And stand a little nearer to the gods.
So this grew in him also, as a bud
Swaying beneath the love-sigh of the spring
Swells out the livelong day, until he found
The looking backward not for any life
Upon this earth. He flung away those dreams
Which lay within the past, as when a rainbow
Fades, leaving one small speck against a cloud,
Pledge of its disappearance, and rose up
To battle manlike—to do what he could
To help his fellows, having in his heart
Those words of Goethe—"One should know his fellows,
And knowing, also learn not to despise"—
A higher wisdom still.

So there is now
In this Alexis better thought in germ
To meet the future with. For from his life

The noonday glare has fled, and left behind
The quieter light that draws the eye, as when
We stand and for a moment face the sun,
Seeming to sink between the hill and sky,
Then turn to view the chasten'd light behind—
Faint harbinger of twilight.   Life to him
Has half unveil'd its meaning, and he sees
No puppet show to make a wrinkle live
About the lip and eye, but earnest work
For earnest men, within whose band must be
No dainty worker, gloved, and ever strong
In idle words, but bare-arm'd fighters, swift
To take advantage of the rising ground
And wave their fellows onward.   He has learnt,
Though he is yet what some call young, that men
Are ever to be on this miraculous earth
To make it better, working hand and brain
To lift it higher, standing firm of foot,
Shoulder to shoulder, striving for all good,
And keeping God and duty in the eye,
As sailors keep the light that marks their port
For guide and haven.   Shame on him if he
Should stand an idle Memnon in the crowd,
Giving responses to each one who strikes,
For the mere whim of hearing sound, and thus
Be jester to his fellows, as a mother
May hum a cradle-song to please her child
Fretful with sleep.   What need of nursery rhyme
In this great age of sounding wire and wheel,
Science and all her handmaids?   Rather toil,
And manly living, manly thought, and all
Those grander interests ever moving on
To where we strive for.   Crude and vaguely dim
Is this life of Alexis yet, but still
It rises slowly upward, as the moon
Bound in a slip of crescent rises up
And shines a silver sickle in the sky.
He may fail in the task of working out
What he has laid before him as a plan,
And sink before the crescent culminate,
And shines an orb, as vessels sink at sea,
Reaching no port.   But now he tears away
The dreamer from his being, calling out
To all his fellows (for in him the wish
To see them reach the purer heights of life
Shoots from the rest, and claims his deepest thought,
As high hills claim the sun) to rise and take
The nobler pathway, working on and up;

Not resting, though the sweat be in our eyes
Blinding our motions, till the brute be shorn
From out our being, and we stand erect,
The earth beneath our feet, the sky above,
And right before us all the nobler path
That narrows not as earthly pathways do,
But ever broadens as it reaches up
Until it ends beside the feet of God.

DAFT AILIE

Daft Ailie cam' in by the auld brig-en'
As the sunlicht, saft an' sweet,
Fell doon on the laigh, white wa's o' the toon,
An' the lang, quate, single street.

It fell on her sair-worn, wrinkled face,
An' on her thin gray hair;
But the licht that lay in her een was a licht
That shouldna hae been there.

An' aye she lookit roun' an' roun',
An' aye a waefu' smile
Lay on her lips, that were thin an' white,
As she mum'led an' sang the while.

Then the weans cam' runnin' oot o' the schule—
The schule had scaled for the nicht—
An' they a' cam' roun' Daft Ailie, an' cried
An' laup in their mad delicht.

Then they took a hand o' ecah ither's han's,
An' made her gang in the ring,
An' they danced roun' aboot her, an' sang a sang
That made the hooses ring.

But when they had danced an' jamp their fill,
They closer an' closer drew,
Cryin', "Ailie, afore we let you oot,
Ye maun make us a bonnie boo."

Then she boo'd to them a' as they stood aroun',
Wi' the boo o' a leddy born,
An' said, "O, weanies, baith ane an' a',
Ye maun come to my bridal the morn.

But I maun away to the auld wud brig,
An' sit 'neath the rowan tree,
An' there I will wait till my bonnie bridegroom
Comes ower to marry me."

"An' what is your bonnie bridegroom like?
Is he strong, an' braid, an' braw?
An' wha is he that will come an' tak'
Auld Ailie frae us a'?"

"Oh, my ain bridegroom is tall an' fair,
An' straucht as a hazel tree,
An' licht is the touch o' his han' in mine,
When he speaks in the gloamin' to me.

An' weel he likes me, I ken, an' weel
Can he whisper his manly voo;
An' weel I like to listen to him—
I can hear his voice the noo.

I saw ane laid oot in white deid-claes,
But my een were unco dim,
An' I couldna hear a word that was said,
Though they tauld me it was him.

But I turn'd my heid frae the cauld, white deid,
That was quate as quate could be,
An' turn'd an' gaed doon to the brig, to wait
For my bridegroom comin' to me.

But I sometimes think he is unco lang,
An' I weary a' the day,
Waitin' here for my bonnie bridegroom to come
An' tak his Ailie away."

"But, Ailie, Ailie," the weans cry out,
"Your hair is gray an' thin,
An' your cheeks are sae sunk that nae bonnie
bridegroom
Will come sic a bride to win."

"O, weanies, weanies! haud a' your tongues;
Ye dinna ken what ye say;
My cheek is reid, an' my e'e is bricht,
For I'm twenty-ane this day.

Put I maun away to the auld wud brig,
An' sit 'neath the rowan tree;

Dinna gang to the schule the morn, but come
An' see my bridegroom an' me."

Then they let her oot o' the ring, an' she gangs
Wi' the same strange, waefu' smile,
Doon the lang quate street, an' she sings a sang
As they follow her a' the while.

But she hauds her way to the en' o' the toon,
An' aye she sorts her hair,
Wi' the same wild licht flaffin' up in her een
That shouldna hae been there.

O weans! O weans! gang a' to your hames,
An' let puir Ailie alane;
She gangs to sit by the auld wud brig
To settle her wan'erin' brain.

She sits for hoors by that auld, frail brig,
Ow'r the braid, deep, dookin' pool,
But a weary, weary wait she will hae,
As she sings her sangs o' dool;

For nae bonnie bridegroom will ever come
To tak' her by the han',
Save ane that comes frae the lan' o' the deid,
When the last lang breath is drawn.

But weel I min that, in a' the toon,
The brawest amang them a'
Was Ailie, what noo gangs frae hoose to hoose,
Giein' ilka body a ca'.

Her cheeks had the saft, sweet bloom o' youth,
An' gowden her lang, thick hair,
An' bricht was the look o' her bonnie blue e'e,
For a sweet life-dream was there.

Ay, weel micht they glance like the simmer licht,
When the sun gangs doon in the west,
For the first pure dream o' love was there,
An' it wadna gie her rest.

But her bridal day cam' quickly roun',
An' mirth an' daffin' was rife,
As we sat ben the room for the hoor to come
That wad see sweet Ailie a wife.

An' O! but she lookit bonnie an' braw
In the flush o' her maiden pride;
An' should I live to a hunner long years,
I shall ne'er see a bonnier bride.

But waes me! whaten a storm cam' on
On that happy afternoon;
The Nith rase up wi' an angry sough,
An' reid wi wrath cam' doon.

The nicht drappit doon, and it grew sae dark
That the hill abune the brae,
Where ye gather in simmer the berries sac black,
Was hid as if ta'en away.

An' never a single star was seen
In the heaven sae dark an' wide,
Yet lichtly the bridegroom cam' doon the path,
To claim his winsome bride.

The lave that were wi' him thet talkit an' lauch'd
In a' their youth an' glee,
Till they cam' to the brig ow'r the dookin' pool,
By the lang, braid rowan tree.

Then the young gudeman that was soon to be
Gaed on't wi' a lichtsome spang;
An' he cried to the lave to come on behin',
For Ailie wad think them lang.

But alake! what a cry gaed up through the nicht,
To the heicht o' the stars aboon—
Sic a cry never rase to their flickerin' licht
Save frae lips o' men that droon.

For half o' the brig had been torn away
By the angry strength o' the spate,
An' the young bridegroom slippit ow'r in the dark
To his quick an' awfu' fate.

They faun' him next day in the minister's holm,
Where the water had flung him oot;
An' they brocht him up to the far toon-en',
But they happit his bridal suit.

They laid him doon, an' they took it aff,
An' dress'd him frae heid to feet
In the dress they put on when we're wedded to death—

The lang, white windin' sheet.

Then Ailie cam' in, but O, what a change
Had come on her through the nicht;
Her gowden hair had a scance o' gray,
An' her een had a strange wild licht.

An' aye she lookit, an' turn'd roun' an' roun'.
While they watch'd her a' the while;
"O, where is my bonnie bridegroom?" she ask'd,
An' her lips had a waefu' smile.

"O Ailie, this is your bonnie bridegroom
That lies in the airms o' death;
Will ye no tak' a look at his face, an' kiss
The lips that hae nae breath?"

"O haud your tongues, haud a' your tongues,
Dinna tell sic lees to me;
I will gang mysel' to the auld wud brig,
My ain bridegroom to see.

I will wait by the rowan tree till he comes—
I ken that he winna be late,
An' I'll sing the sangs I hae heard him sing,
They will cheer me as I wait."

So she turn'd an' gaed doon to the auld wud brig,
As ye see her gang the noo,
Wi' the same waefu' smile on her thin white lips,
An' the sorrow upon her broo.

An' aye she wan'ers aboot the brig,
Ye may see her late an' sune,
Still waitin' for him wha is in his grave,
An' the green, green grass abune.

Then, weanies, weanies, gang a' to your hames,
An' let puir Ailie be;
Ye little ken what a weird she drees,
By the auld braid rowan tree.

MAY MIDDLETON'S TAM

Frae the schulehoose that sat at the heid o' the green,
To the fit o' the toon where the smiddy was seen—

Frae the narrow close mooth to the hoose on the brae,
Where the weans at odd times met to scamper an' play—
Frae the heid o' the parish to a' the laigh boun',
In a word, tak' at ance the hale country-side roun',
Frae the laird to the joiner that cooper'd a tram,
A' had an ill word o' May Middleton's Tam.

He had gleg een, an' mooth that was aye on the gape,
But his face for sax months hadna lookit on saip;
An' Nature hersel' had supplied him wi' shoon,
Sae waukit he'd dee maist afore they wore dune.
His knees play'd bo-keek through a rive in his breeks,
For his mither lang sync had lost a' faith in steeks;
But he scamper'd aboot fu' o' glee as a lamb—
'Od, an awfu' ill plague was May Middleton's Tam.

The back o' his han' was as broon as a taid,
An', as he had grown since his jacket was made,
The half o' his airm to the elbow was bare,
An' a scrimpit bit sark half in tatters was there;
While, what wi' the dichtin' his nose noo and thaun,
The tae sleeve was bricht as the lid o' a can—
There was nae washin' day to mak' dirt tak' a dwam
But wear on an' wear dune wi' May Middleton's Tam.

Had a stane been sent through ony window within
A mile frae his hoose, or some mischief been dune;
The mooth o' the pump stappit up, or a score,
Or the heid o' a man drawn wi' chalk on the door;
A deuk or a hen gotten deid, or a wean
Knockit into the siver when flowin' wi' rain—
"Wha could hae dune this?"   An' the answer aye cam'—
"Deil tak' him, wha else but May Middleton's Tam!"

He stole a' the bools frae the rest o' the weans,
An' pelted the big anes wha fash'd him wi' stanes;
He knockit aff bonnets, he ran ahint gigs,
He climb'd up on cairts, an' he ran alang brigs;
He jaggit the cuddy o' big ragman Jock
Till the croons that it made nearly frichten'd the folk;
An' yet, at the schule, nane could say verse or psalm
Freer aff heart an' tongue than May Middleton's Tam.

He was heid o' a' ill baith at mornin' an' late,
Sae that maist o' the folk wish'd him oot o' the gate,
But Birky, the maister, wha keepit the schule,
Said, aye when they ca'd him a rascal an' fule—
'There is something in Tam, if ye just wait a wee,

That will mak' ye a' glower, ill an' a' though he be."
But I wat Birky's faith was consider'd a sham,
For the deevil's ain bird was May Middleton's Tam.

He was twice carried hame wi' a cut in his heid,
Ony ithers but him 'twad hae streekit them deid;
But the eggs o' a corbie or piat to him
Were something worth while to risk life for an' limb.
He was catch'd by the miller gaun doon the mill race,
A' the hairm was a fricht, an' less dirt on the face;
An' thrice he was brocht half-droon'd oot o' the dam—
Od, the hangman was sure o' May Middleton's Tam.

His mither, puir woman, did a' that she could
To keep him in boun's, as a richt mither should;
But ance ower the door, she was oot o' his thocht,
An' a crony gaun by he was ready for ocht.
Then bare-leggit weans at the door micht look oot
To get, in the by-gaun, a push or a cloot;
But they took to their heels wi' a jump like a ram—
They a' stood in fear o' May Middleton's Tam.

But ill as he was, he grew up stoot an' steive,
Braid shuider'd, big baned, an' a dawd o' a neive;
Then he wrocht noo an' thaun, when the simmer cam roun',
Howin' turnips, or drivin' some nowte to the toon;
But as yet wark an' him werena like to agree,
A' his talk was 'boot sailors an' storms at the sea,
Till ae day he left withoot tears or a qualm,
An' the village was rid o' May Middleton's Tam.

Years gaed by, an' nae word cam' frae Tam, till at last
His mither hersel' thocht that a' hope was past,
When ae day the postman gaed in at the door—
A thing the douce neebours had ne'er ken'd afore;
But aye after that a blin' man micht hae seen
That her hoose an' hersel' were mair cheerfu' an' bien.
"Lod," quo' ane, as she lean'd hersel' 'gainst the door jamb,
"Has ocht been sent hame by her ne'er-dae-weel Tam?"

But a greater surprise they were a' yet to get,
When the handy bit farm o' Whaupfields was to let;
Neebours ran into neebours wi' weans in their arm,
Cryin', "Help us, May Middleton's Tam's got the farm;"
An' after awee, it was heard Tam himsel'
Wad be back in his ain native clachan to dwell.
He cam', an' the doors were as fu' as could cram
Wi' folk keen to look at May Middleton's Tam.

But losh? what a braw, strappin' fellow they saw,
Broon-faced, and a beard that was black as a craw;
Lang, lang did they glower, till the blacksmith said "Fegs,
What a change since he broke wi' a stane Whaupey's legs."
Here it cam' to his min' o' the wark on the farm,
Sae he added, "But Tam never did ony harm."
Then he ended by makin' a sort o' salaam
Doon the street to the hoose o' May Middleton's Tam.

But when ance Tam was into his farm, an' had made
A' things snod, an' his mither as mistress array'd,
He tea'd a' the neebours, and tellt them what wark
He had makin' a fortune that cost him much cark.
Then he turn'd roun' to Birky, the maister, wha sat
By his side, lookin' up as if prood aboot that,
An' said, clappin' his back, "Here's your health in a dram,
For ye aye took the pairt o' May Middleton's Tam."

An' frae that day to this ilka body speaks weel
O' Tam, while they praise his guid praties an' meal;
An' mithers, who ance could hae seen his neck thrawn,
Gie him days at the hay when there's ower muckle mawn.
E'en the landlord himsel' comes an' cries, unco big,
"Here, boy, come an' haud Mr. Middleton's gig."
For since things took a turn, an' his guid fortune cam',
He is noo nae mair ken'd as May Middleton's Tam.

JOHN KEATS

There be more things within that far-off breast,
Whereon the flowers grow,
Of the boy poet, in his Roman rest,
Than hearts like ours can know.

He slumbers, but his sleep hath not our fears,
For all aside is thrown;
And from the gateway of his tombèd years
A power is moving on.

And in that power is hid a voice that speaks
To hearts that throb and rise
From common earth, and worship that which seeks
The wider sympathies.

For he is silent not; and from the bounds

Wherein his footsteps move
Come, like the wind at morn, all summer sounds
Of boyhood thought and love.

So he to us is as an oracle
Whose words bedrip with youth;
The latest spirit, bathing in the well
Of Pagan shape and truth.

A passionate existence which we scan;
But first must lay aside
The rougher thinking that belongs to man,
And take the unsettled pride

Of eager youth and fancy, and a strength
Misled by the fond zeal
For Grecian look and light, yet found at length
The power to touch and feel.

So, taking this into thy thought, ye trace
His wealth of opening lore;
He bursts upon you with his freshest grace,
And moves a man no more—

But a bright shadow in the heart's expanse
Crown'd with the tenderest rays
Of love, and thought of as the far-off glance
Of early summer days.

So bring him from beneath the sky of Rome,
From all her youngest flowers.
I weep that there his dust should find a home,
And all his spirit ours!

But no! ye cannot; for a bond he keeps
Whose ties are firmly strung—
The lone yet passionate heart of Shelley sleeps
Beside the dust he sung.

And it were vain to leave him there and foil
His rest—so let them sleep
Within the silence of that glorious soil,
Whose inspirations steep

Their songs in colours like the summer boughs,
Whose freshness ever strives,
And blooms, like asphodels, upon the brows
Of two immortal lives.

And there they sleep, as if their fates had said
They shall not sleep alone;
The singer and the sung must fill one bed,
And make their ashes one.

And so it is; and through the years that roll,
That sepulchre of theirs
Is as a passionate and wish'd-for goal
To which all thought repairs—

While in our hearts, as is their dust at Rome,
Their spirits feel no wrong;
But shine to us like gods serenely from
The Pantheon of Song.

THE ENGINE

Hurrah! for the mighty engine,
As he bounds along his track:
Hurrah, for the life that is in him,
And his breath so thick and black.
And hurrah for our fellows, who in their need
Could fashion a thing like him—
With a heart of fire, and a soul of steel,
And a Samson in every limb.

Ho! stand from that narrow path of his,
Lest his gleaming muscles smite,
Like the flaming sword the archangel drew
When Eden lay wrapped in night;
For he cares, not he, for a paltry life
As he rushes along to the goal,
It but costs him a shake of his iron limb,
And a shriek from his mighty soul.

Yet I glory to think that I help to keep
His footsteps a little in place,
And he thunders his thanks as he rushes on
In the lightning speed of his race,
And I think that he knows when he looks at me,
That, though made of clay as I stand,
I could make him as weak as a three hours' child
With a paltry twitch of my hand.

But I trust in his strength, and he trusts in me,

Though made but of brittle clay,
While he is bound up in the toughest of steel,
That tires not night or day;
But for ever flashes, and stretches, and strives,
While he shrieks in his smoky glee—
Hurrah for the puppets that, lost in their thoughts,
Could rub the lamp for me!

O that some Roman—when Rome was great—
Some quick, light Greek or two—
Could come from their graves for one half-hour
To see what my fellows can do;
I would take them with me on this world's wild steed,
And give him a little rein;
Then rush with his clanking hoofs through space,
With a wreath of smoke for his mane.

I would say to them as they shook in their fear,
"Now what is your paltry book,
Or the Phidian touch of the chisel's point,
That can make the marble look,
To this monster of ours, that for ages lay
In the depths of the dreaming earth,
Till we brought him out with a cheer and a shout,
And hammer'd him into birth?"

Clank, clank went the hammer in dusty shops,
The forge-flare went to the sky,
While still, like the monster of Frankenstein's,
This great wild being was nigh;
Till at length he rose up in his sinew and strength,
And our fellows could see with pride
Their grimy brows and their bare, slight arms,
In the depths of his glancing side.

Then there rose to their lips a dread question of fear—
"Who has in him the nerve to start
In this mass a soul that will shake and roll
A river of life to his heart?"
Then a pigmy by jerks went up his side,
Flung a globe of fire in his breast,
And cities leapt nearer by hundred of miles
At the first wild snort from his chest.

Then away he rush'd to his mission of toil,
Wherever lay guiding rods,
And the work he could do at each throb of his pulse
Flung a blush on the face of the gods.

And Atlas himself, when he felt his weight,
Bent lower his quaking limb,
Then shook himself free from this earth, and left
The grand old planet to him.

But well can he bear it, this Titan of toil,
When his pathway yields to his tread;
And the vigour within him flares up to its height,
Till the smoke of his breath grows red;
Then he shrieks in delight, as an athlete might,
When he reaches his wild desire,
And from head to heel, through each muscle of steel,
Runs the cunning and clasp of the fire.

Or, see how he tosses aside the night,
And roars in his thirsty wrath,
While his one great eye gleams white with rage
At the darkness that muffles his path;
And lo! as the pent-up flame of his heart
Flashes out from behind its bars,
It gleams like a bolt flung from heaven, and rears
A ladder of light to the stars.

Talk of the sea flung back in its wrath
By a line of unyielding stone,
Or the slender clutch of a thread-like bridge,
That knits two valleys in one!
Talk of your miracle-working wires,
And their world-embracing force,
But himmel! give me the bits of steel
In the mouth of the thunder-horse!

Ay, give me the beat of his fire-fed breast,
And the shake of his giant frame,
And the sinews that work like the shoulders of Jove
When he launches a bolt of flame;
And give me that Lilliput rider of his,
Stout and wiry and grim,
Who can vault on his back as he puffs his pipe,
And whisk the breath from him.

Then hurrah for our mighty engine, boys;
He may roar and fume along
For a hundred years ere a poet arise
To shrine him in worthy song;
Yet if one with the touch of the gods on his lips,
And his heart beating wildly and quick,
Should rush into song at this demon of ours,

Let him sing, too, the shovel and pick.

THE CUCKOO

Amid the sound of picks to-day,
And shovels rasping on the rail,
A sweet voice came from far away,
From out a gladly greening vale.

My mate look'd up in some surprise;
I half stopp'd humming idle rhyme:
Then said, the moisture in my eyes,
"The cuckoo, Jack, for the first time."

How sweet he sang! I could have stood
For hours, and heard that simple strain;
An early gladness throng'd my blood,
And brought my boyhood back again.

The primrose took a deeper hue,
The dewy grass a greener look;
The violet wore a deeper blue,
A lighter music led the brook.

Each thing to its own depth was stirr'd,
Leaf, flower, and heaven's moving cloud,
As still he piped, that stranger bird,
His mellow May-song clear and loud.

Would I could see him as he sings,
When, as if thought and act were one,
He came; the gray on neck and wings
Turn'd white against the happy sun.

I knew his well-known sober flight,
That boyhood made so dear to me;
And, blessings on him! he stopp'd in sight,
And sang where I could hear and see.

Two simple notes were all he sang,
And yet my manhood fled away;
Dear God! The earth is always young,
And I am young with it to-day.

A wondrous realm of early joy
Grew all around as I became

Among my mates a bearded boy,
That could have wept but for the shame.

For all my purer life, now dead,
Rose up, fair-fashion'd, at the call
Of that gray bird, whose voice had shed
The charm of boyhood over all.

O early hopes and sweet spring tears!
That heart has never known its prime
That stands without a tear and hears
The cuckoo's voice for the first time.

LOOK TO THE EAST

The dead man came from out the grave,
He grasp'd my hand, and said, "Be brave."

I cried, "So very far away,
Yet thou hast sympathy with clay."

He said, "What would it profit me
To turn from thy humanity?"

"Alas!" I sigh'd, "I am but dust,
And the old failing of mistrust

Comes up within me, and I fear
I falter with no purpose here."

The dead man stood like one who saith
A prayer, then ask'd, "Hast thou no faith?"

I look'd at him; within his eyes
The tears rose up as in surprise.

Then I made answer to his thought—
"Thou knowest all, and I know nought."

Across his brow a shade of pain
Pass'd, but to leave it clear again.

He ask'd, reproach his voice within,
"Art thou, too, smitten with that sin

Which looks before this life, to seek,

What God himself will never speak,

Until this death we paint so grim,
Guide thee through the dread grave to Him?"

I bow'd my head as if in shame
To hear the dead man's gentle blame.

Then, sweet and low, he spoke again,
"Hast thou faith in thy fellow men?"

"Yea," I return'd, "for still my kind
Toil to leave something good behind,

Which, in the unborn after years,
Will ripen kindly with their peers."

I paused, and he, when this was said,
Laid one soft hand upon my head,

And thus made answer ere I wist,
"Behind thy kind work God and Christ,

And all the marvels men can do,
Are but the shadow of these Two.

Whom, then, deserves thy greater trust,
God, Christ, or men who are but dust?

"I knelt down at the dead man's feet;
His tears fell on me soft and sweet.

He raised me up, and hand in hand
We stood, as two together stand.

Then breast to breast, within my ear
He whisper'd words of love and cheer.

Such words a living mortal may
Not whisper, but the dead can say.

Then said, as he touch'd lips and eyes,
"Look to the east; the sun will rise."

I turn'd; my soul was strong again
To trust God, Christ, and toiling men.

And still when doubt wakes from its rest

That dead man clasps me to his breast,

And soul to soul like friends respond:
Mine from this earth; his from beyond.

Mine sighs, "I falter;" his replies,
"Look to the east; the sun will rise."

THE DEIL'S STANE

"In the very centre of the deep gorge of this linn is an immense boulder, estimated at thirty tons weight. It is a mass of water-worn granite, probably from the Isle of Arran, as its granulated particles seem to be precisely of the same character of those that compose the granite of Goatfell. It must have been conveyed in the age of the northern drift, or dropped from the base of some massive iceberg as it sailed the waters that erst covered these heights. It is rounded like an egg, and has a belt of finer grain begirding its bulk like an iron hoop around a barrel."—Simpson's "Voice from the Desert." Such is the account given by the late Dr. Simpson of Sanquhar; but in the neighbourhood the boulder in question is known by the dignified appellation of the "Deil's Stane." How it came to get such a title I have not been able to learn. Long ago, a pedlar was murdered near the spot for the sake of the petty wares he traded with among the hills. They still show you his blood in the channel of the Orchard burn, close to where the stone is lying. This, like all other blood shed in like circumstances, will not wash out. I have in the following poem, with the license usually granted to rhymers, wandered from received tradition in order to "point a moral and adorn a tale."*

"O whaur hae ye been, my bonnie,
bonnie bairns,
Sae lang awa' frae me?
Come in, come in, for I'm weary to hae
Wee Jeanie upon my knee.

I lookit lang doon the howms o' the Craw'ck,
Where the fairies by munelicht play,
Then up to the daisies that grow sae white
On the side o' the Carco brae.

For I thocht that ye micht be pooin' flooers,
An' weavin' them into a croon
For wee Jeanie's heid! but I saw na ane,
Though I lookit roun' an roun'."

"O, grannie, grannie, we werena there,
Nor yet in the howms doon by;
For we sat by the edge o' the Orchard burn,
An' we heard the cushie's cry.

Then we frichten'd the troots oor wee white feet,

As we paidled up the burn,
Till they splutter'd to win frae oor sicht in the broo,
Wi' mony a jouk an' turn.

But at last we waded nae farrer up,
But set wee Jeanie her lane,
Wi' a bunch o' primroses in her han',
On the tap o' the deil's big stane."

"O bairnies, bairnies, what is't ye say?
An' what does your grannie hear?
What made ye gang up to the deil's big stane—
That place sae dark an' drear?

Alake, alake, when the clock strikes twal,
What soun's an' what sichts are there;
When the howlet flaps wi' an eerie cry,
Through the woods o' Knockenhair!

Then chields that hae drucken baith lang an' late
At their howfs in Sanquhar toon,
As they staucher by hear the paidlar's cry,
An' the big stane rumblin' doon.

But here, as we're a' sittin' roun' the fire,
An' wee Jeanie upon my knee,
I will tell ye the tale o' the paidlar's death,
As my mither tauld it to me.

Wee Mungo Girr was an auld, auld man,
Wi' a hump upon his back;
But fu' yauld was he at speelin' a brae
To a herd's house wi' his pack.

For the clink o' siller put smiles on his face,
An' a gleg look in his e'e;
But wae to the greed that brocht on his doom,
An' the death he had to dee.

He keepit his purse in a stockin' fit—
A purse fu' heavy an' lang;
An' ilka mornin' he counted it ow'r,
For fear that it micht gang wrang.

An' aye as the shillin's play'd slip aff his loof,
An' jingled into the lave,
He scartit his heid, an' he hotch'd an' lauch'd
Till he scarce could weel behave.

O, bairnies, bairnies, the love o' gowd
Turns into an awfu' sin,
For the heart grows hard, an' lies dead in the breast,
Like the bouk o' my nieve o' whin.

An' we canna look straicht in oor neebor's face.
For oor human love gets thrawn;
An' we canna look up to the sky abune,
For oor heid is downward drawn.

Sae Mungo, the paidlar, gaed aye half boo'd,
Comin' up or gaun doon a brae;
For the luve o' the siller he liket sae weel
Was in him by nicht an' day.

An' weel could he manage to wheedle an' sell,
To the lassies oot on the hill,
A brooch for their shawls, or a finger ring,
That was gowd in their simple skill.

But alake for the greed that hung ow'r his heid
To bring him meikle woe,
As a thunder cloud rests on the high Bale Hill,
An' darkens the fields below.

But I'll tell ye the tale that my mither tauld,
When I was a toddlin' wean;
It will mak' ye nae mair tak' the Orchard burn
To sit on the deil's big stane.

Ae afternoon, as Mungo, half boo'd,
Held alang steep Carco brae,
Croon into himsel', for his heart was glad
Ow'r the bargains he'd made that day;

A' at ance, afore ever he kent, a han'
Touch'd the hump that was on his back,
An', turnin' roun', no a yaird frae himsel'
Was a man that was cled in black."

"O, Mungo, Mungo, pit doon yer pack,
An' sell to me," said he,
"A necklace for ane o' the witches o' Craw'ck,
Wha has dune gude wark for me."

Then the paidlar open'd his pack in a glint,
An' oot wi' the wanted gear;

"A shillin's the price;" said the man in black—
"O, Mungo, your shillin's here."

Then he slippit the shillin' into his han',
An' steppit alang the brae;
But what made Mungo jump up an' dance,
Like schule weans at their play?

Ay, weel micht he jump like daft, for he saw
A joyfu' sicht, I wis;
Instead o' the shillin' a guinea lay there,
That by nae kent law was his.

Yet he row'd it up in a cloot by itsel',
For fear it micht grow dim,
An' never let on to the neebors he met
O' the luck that had fa'en to him.

The next time gangin' ow'r Carco heicht,
A han' was laid on his back,
An', lookin' aroun', no a yaird frae himsel'
Was the same man cled in black.

Then the paidlar's heart sank doon like a stane
As he thocht to himsel', nae doot,
He has come again to tak' back his ain,
That I canna dae withoot.

But he juist said, " Mungo, come doon wi'
your pack,
An' sell me richt speedily
A necklace for ane o' the witches o' Craw'ck,
Wha has dune gude wark for me."

Then Mungo, richt happy that this was a',
Cam' oot wi' the wanted gear;
A shillin's the price;" said the man in black—
"O, Mungo, your shillin's here."

Then he slippit the shillin' into his loof,
While the paidlar steekit his een;
Nor open'd them up till the man in black
Was naewhere to be seen.

Then he keekit into his loof, an' there
Lay anither gowd guinea bricht;
Sae he row'd it up wi' the first in a cloot,
An' thocht that a' was richt.

The next time gangin' ow'r Carco hill,
A han' was laid on his back,
An', lookin roun', no a yaird frae himsel'
Was the same man cled in black.

But a frichtfu' look was upon his broo,
As he leant against a stane
That Mungo had never seen there afore,
An' thirty tons if ane.

A fear lay cauld at the paidlar's heart,
As he sank doon on his knee—
"Come ye here to work me scaith or ill,
Or to buy a necklace frae me?"

The froon grew black on the stranger's broo
As he cried, like a thunder-peal,
"A necklace o' fire for the neck o' him
Wha cheats baith man an' deil."

Then the lowe cam' oot at his mouth an' een,
On ilk side o' his heid grew a horn;
As he seized the paidlar an' whirl'd him ow'r
The hill wi' a lauch o' scorn.

Doon, doon the hill, as ye ca' a gird,
Gaed Mungo, flung by the deil;
An' doon row'd that big stane after him,
As steady as some mill-wheel.

Then, keep us a'! what a soun' cam' up
Wi' the paidlar's deein' cry;
It gaed doon the Craw'ck an' doon the Nith,
An' awa' ow'r the hills oot by.

The big stane fell in the Orchard burn,
It lies there till this day;
An' still at its fit is the paidlar's bluid,
That winna was away.

O, bairnies, bairnies, when ye grow up
To be lads an' lasses fair,
Keep min' o' the death o' Mungo Girr,
An' aye deal frank an' fair.

An' bairnies, be sure an' keep this in min',
For I canna lang be here,

That the deil's big stane is on ilka ane's back
Wha has love for notch but gear.

THE MOTHER AND THE ANGEL

"I want my child," the mother said, as through
The deep sweet air of purple-breathing morn
She rose mid clouds of most celestial hue,
By the soft strength of angels' wings upborne.

Then he who bore her to her heavenly rest
Drew back the hand that hid her weeping eyes,
And said, "I cannot alter the request
Of him whose glory lights the earth and skies.

For ere I came, and, as I paused again,
To hear His omnipresent words, He said,
'Take thou the root, but let the bud remain,
To perfect into blossom in its stead.'

And so I bear thee, that in our sweet land
You may be one of our immortal kind,
With not one task but to reach forth thy hand
And guide the footsteps of thy child behind."

He ceased, and winging, reach'd those realms on high,
Whose lustre we half see through stars below,
And all the light that fills our earthly sky
Is but a shadow to its mighty glow.

Now whether that the mother in this light
Stood yearning for her treasure in our hands,
Or whether God saw fitting in His might
To reunite again the broken bands

We know not; but when night had come at last,
And wore to clasp the first embrace of day.
An angel enter'd, though the door was fast,
And all unseen took what we held away.

One took the mother from all earthly claim,
From out the bounds of life and all its harms;
But still I think 'twas God Himself that came,
And took the child and laid it in her arms.

God said, "I take my stand behind
Men, Nature, and the shaping mind.

And cry, 'The open secret lies
To him who reads with proper eyes.'"

Then thought came boldly forth, and lent
Its strength to conquer what was meant,

The Hebrew with his passionate heart
Came on, and solved it part by part.

The high Greek saw, but turn'd aside,
With beauty walking by his side.

At last came One, upon whose head
The light of God Himself was shed.

He read the secret, and divine
For ever after grew each line.

Then sullen cycles follow'd Him,
In which His reading would not dim.

The ages sped, but still took heed
To wait, and mould a band at need,

Whose worded cunning might lay bare
The omnific secret everywhere.

Stern Dante saw it, though his face
Was darken'd by the nether place.

Next Shakespeare, who, before his kind,
Stept with it forming in his mind.

Then Milton, blind and old in years,
Stood nearer to it than his peers.

Later a Goethe wander'd by,
To see it only with his eye.

At last the nineteenth century came,
With railway track and furnace flame,

At which, as at a mighty need,
Men's thoughts flew into headlong speed.

Then one rose up, whose northern ire
Smote shams, like sudden bursts of fire.

A rouglily-block'd Apollo, strong
To pierce the coiling Python, Wrong.

Last Science, waking from her sleep,
Sent forth her thought to sound the deep,

But, like the dove sent from the ark,
It came back, having found no mark,

Then she stood up and proudly said,
"The open secret is not read."

O foolish one! Wrap weeds of shame
Around that keen device you claim.

"Behold!" cries God, "I stand and teach,
The open secret is for each.

I slip my own wide soul behind
Men, nature, and the shaping mind,

And he who can unite these three,
Until they lose themselves in me,

The same hath in him, night and day,
The open secret I display."

THE SPIRIT OF THE WATERS

How quick, and yet how soft
Comes the moonlight from aloft—
From the happy starry skies,
Like the smiles of angels' eyes,
Flinging all the silvery whiteness
Of its purity and brightness
On the stream
That dances up with laughter
As the wavelets follow after
Each other in the glee
Of a pleasant symphony.

I stand upon the bridge,
Leaning on its narrow ledge,
Keeping watch with dreaming eye
On the river gliding by,
Till I fancy from the deeps,
Where the moonlight sits and sleeps,
I can hear a whisper say—
"Come away, come away,
Come, and never know decay,
Come, and rest beneath the stream,
And for ever smile and dream.
Through the night and sunny day,
Dream of things with joyance rife,
Dream of all that makes this life
Bright and gay.
While the waters ebb and creep
With their murmurs o'er thy sleep—
While the moonlight from above
Rains the pale wealth of her love
On the wave, on thy grave—
Come away."

And I feel a strong desire
Burning in me to inquire
What this gentle sprite may be,
Who sings such a song to me
From the stream.
For, as I hear his lay,
Like a voice from far away,
With its burden, "Come away,"
I can reason thus how sweet
To let all the waters meet
O'er the weary, dreamy head;
And to sink, as in a bed,
In the tide, and there to lie
All the night and watch the sky;
Or sleep, sleep, sleep,
While the breezes come and creep—
And what mortal would not sleep
To such soothing lullaby,
While the happy moon above
Would fling down her wealth of love
On the wave, on my grave,
On my dream.

That was Nottman waving at me,
But the steam fell down, so you could not see;
He is out to-day with the fast express,
And running a mile in the minute, I guess.

Danger? none in the least, for the way
Is good, though the curves are sharp as you say,
But bless you, when trains are a little behind,
They thunder around them—a match for the wind.

Nottman himself is a devil to drive,
But cool and steady, and ever alive
To whatever danger is looming in front,
When a train has run hard to gain time for a shunt.

But he once got a fear, though, that shook him with pain,
Like sleepers beneath the weight of a train.
I remember the story well, for, you see,
His stoker, Jack Martin, told it to me.

Nottman had sent down the wife for a change
To the old folks living at Riverly Grange,
A quiet sleepy sort of a town,
Save when the engines went up and down.

For close behind it the railway ran
In a mile of a straight if a single span;
Three bridges were over the straight, and between
Two the distant signal was seen.

She had with her her boy—a nice little chit
Full of romp and mischief, and childish wit,
And every time that we thunder'd by,
Both were out on the watch for Nottman and I.

"Well, one day," said Jack, "on our journey down,
Coming round on the straight at the back of the town,
I saw right ahead, in front of our track,
In the haze on the rail something dim-like and black.

"I look'd over at Nottman, but ere I could speak,
He shut off the steam, and with one wild shriek,
A whistle took to the air with a bound;
But the object ahead never stirr'd at the sound.

"In a moment he flung himself down on his knee,

Leant over the side of the engine to see,
Took one look, then sprung up, crying, breathless and pale,
Brake, Jack, it is some one asleep on the rail!'

"The rear brakes were whistled on in a trice
While I screw'd on the tender brake firm as a vice,
But still we tore on with this terrible thought
Sending fear to our hearts—'Can we stop her or not?'

"I took one look again, then sung out to my mate,
'We can never draw up, we have seen it too late.'
When, sudden and swift, like the change in a dream,
Nottman drew back the lever, and flung on the steam.

"The great wheels stagger'd and span with the strain,
While the spray from the steam fell around us like rain,
But we slacken'd our speed, till we saw with a wild
Throb at the heart, right before us,—a child!

"It was lying asleep on the rail, with no fear
Of the terrible death that was looming so near;
The sweat on us both broke as cold as the dew
Of death as we question'd—'What can we do?'

"It was done—swift as acts that take place in a dream—
Nottman rush'd to the front and knelt down on the beam,
Put one foot in the couplings; the other he kept
Right in front of the wheel for the child that still slept.

"'Saved!' I burst forth, my heart leaping with pride,
For one touch of the foot sent the child to the side,
But Nottman look'd up, his lips white as with foam,
'My God, Jack,' he cried, 'It's my own little Tom!'

"He shrunk, would have slipp'd, but one grasp of my hand,
Held him firm till the engine was brought to a stand,
Then I heard from behind a shriek take to the air,
And I knew that the voice of a mother was there.

"The boy was all right, had got off with a scratch:
He had crept through the fence in his frolic to watch
For his father; but, wearied with mischief and play,
Had fallen asleep on the rail where he lay.

"For days after that on our journey down,
Ere we came to the straight at the back of the town,
As if the signal were up with its gleam
Of red, Nottman always shut off the steam."

SUMMER INVOCATION

Come forth, and bring with thee a mind
That rises to the poet's mood;
And leave the village far behind,
And spend an hour within the wood;

For there the flowers begin to peer—
Sweet primroses that ever seem
The glowing eyes of the New Year
Lit up with Summer and her dream.

And violets that scarce are seen
Until you stoop, with patient eye,
And see them in their lowly mien,
Blue droplets shaken from the sky.

Come forth, so that thy soul again
May talk a while with quiet things
That living far apart from men,
Have in them love's untamper'd springs.

I heard the voice—like one who dreams
I went forth, having in my breast
A stirring quiet, like the streams
When pausing for a little rest.

I reach the wood, and all around
The yearly mystery of birth
Unfolds itself without a sound,
And broadens over all the earth.

The buds in virgin greenness burst
And swell beneath the kindly skies
All pure as when they grew at first,
Upon the boughs in Paradise.

The grass grows up, and in the wind
Waves tiny fingers to and fro,
As if distraught to probe and find
The secret of its life below.

I lay myself within the shade,
I close my eyes, but in my ear
Voices and many sounds invade,

With whispers which I like to hear.

For strange it is that as I lie,
The wind, that leaves no footstep, seems
The spirit of that melody
Which gave my boyhood all its dreams.

And as I listen, like a song
Dear lips have sung in other years,
There comes, with fragrance pure and strong,
From pent-up sources—sweetest tears.

I weep, and yet I know not why,
For joy is hand in hand with pain;
Perchance it is to think how dry
Our hearts remain for all such rain.

Or maybe of that other time,
When youth uprising boldly said,
"I will sow seed in noble prime,"
Alas! and tears have grown instead.

But still, as here I lie to-day,
Seeing the new life quicken all,
The old hard feeling slips away,
And I am under softer thrall,

I look, and from the slightest thing
That God has fashion'd with His hand:
New thoughts and meanings upward spring
That are not hard to understand.

And as I think and slowly slip
Backward to all that early time,
I feel a prayer upon my lip,
And in my heart a holier rhyme,

Until all freshen'd, as with dews
That fall not from the sky above,
But from some angel's eyes; I lose
The old self in a nobler love.

And I can look, as now I view
The buds and grass, and singing birds,
On men, and know their purpose too,
And wed my thoughts to nobler words.

I leave the wood all firm and bold,

And whisper as through fields I pass—
"Dear Heaven, that heart is never old
That takes an interest in the grass—

That hears in every lowly thing
That spring has waken'd with her call
A God-taught melody, that sings,
And gives a key-note unto all."

READING THE BOOK

I sat by night and read the Book,
Till doubt was mingled with my look,

And dimness lay before my eyes,
As mists in hollows form and rise.

"So dark, so very dark," I said,
And shut the Book and bow'd my head;

Then lo!   I felt a wondrous light
Behind me, making all things bright;

While a clear voice, like some refrain,
Said—"Ope the Book, and read again."

I open'd up its leaves, and lo!
Each page was living with the glow

Of some great Presence undefin'd,
Yet standing in its place behind.

Methought that as I read the Word
Each leaf turn'd of its own accord,

And all the meaning fair and clear,
As pebbles through the stream appear,

Lay to my eyes, that saw beneath
Each sentence lie without its sheath.

I raised my head, and spoke in fear—
"This is God's Book, and very clear."

Then, lo! the light behind me fled,
But left a clear, sweet voice that said—

"Read thou not like to him who sees
Evolving mists of mysteries,

But like to him whose heart perceives
God's finger turning o'er the leaves!"

SONNETS TO A PICTURE

I

He sleeps; the inner agony hath pass'd
With the sure dawn that slowly climbs the east;
The night wherein man saw Him not hath ceas'd,
And sleep is on that glorious face at last.
But pain still lingers there, though faint and worn,
Upon the grandest of all brows, whereon
It makes its latest stand to be o'erthrown,
By the sunrise of Love's eternal morn.
It is no painter's touch! beneath those eyes
The mission and the Cross rise slowly up;
Death with them with the dregs that He must sup,
And sorrow with her choruses of sighs.
And over all a halo from above,
God's Signet on His Masterpiece of Love.

II

The splendid demon with the lurid eyes,
Wherein, as when a serpent bites its coil
Nearing its death—hate having felt its foil,
Turns back upon itself before it dies.
He sits; one massive evil, huge of limb,
With hand still clench'd as with the wish to slay;
While those dark brows for ever waste away
With their own anger as they glare at Him.
That beauty which repels nor draws us nigher
Clothes him as with a raiment. We draw near,
Drawn, yet held back as by instinctive fear—
As if a tongue from that dread crown of fire
Could leap to meet us, like a stroke from fate,
And blast us with the poison of its hate.

III

A Faust in colours with the good and ill
For ever at their conflict, dumb of speech,
Nor drawing gladiator-like to each,
But armour'd in the panoply of will.
The ages with their trailing shadows wait,
And Time, the white field-marshal with keen eyes.
Surveys the struggle, while the passive skies
Bend and come nearer as if drawn by fate.
Thou thinkest God has hid himself, but, lo!
His awful shadow, or a part, at least,
Of that which is His shadow, dawns to view
In the young day, that, with its plumes aglow,
All silently behind the silent Two
Climbs the blue stair-way of the one-starr'd east.

SONNETS TO A PICTURE

I

He kneels, his knee drawn down to kindred dust,
For all is earth within him, from those eyes
Wherein a noble nature fallen lies,
To the lean hands that clutch, as clutch they must,
The muck-rake of this world, for unto him
His heaven is on a level with his soul,
That, blind, can see no higher, purer goal
Than in the gold that glitters but to dim.
Jewels that tarnish, honours that take wing
A moment after, luring shapes that sink
To leave the grinning skull whose sockets blink
Derision sharper than the viper's sting,
And Vanity, by hollow whispers nursed,
Blowing her bubbles, which ere caught have burst.

II

Above him, yet he sees him not, there bends
Compassion and Divinity in one,
The Christ of time, earth, heaven, and the sun,
Of the soul's soul, and all that upward tends.
In His right hand he holds a crown of thorns,
Sorrow's own symbol, and the other lies
Almost upon him, while behind him mourns
His better angel with entreating eyes.

Thou toiler after things that will not live!
Look but once upward, that thy soul may see
The sadden'd splendour of that glorious face,
Then lift thyself against that hand, and give
Thy better angel one sweet tear to place
Within the very sight of God from thee.

III

Thou gazest and the picture fades away
Like visions after sleep. But unto thee
One thing remaineth which thou still canst see,
Like midnight meteors when they flash astray.
It is the woven crown of thorns, and lo,
Behind it, on thy dim and awe-struck sight
There rises up a cross of pale sad light
That slowly deepens till its very glow
Reaches thy inmost soul that, kneeling down
Beneath a sorrow which all speech but mars,
Sees, as a glory rises in the night,
Through the rough circlet of the thorny crown
Another issue forth that to the sight
Becomes a blinding splendour thick with stars.

THE RED LEAF

Have you so forgot the time, dear love,
When we sat by the stream in the wood
With our hearts as bright as the sky above,
Talking as lovers should?
And we whisper'd to each of that happy day—
Looking forward is so sweet—
But still as the moments sped away
The red leaf fell at our feet.

The birds were out on the leafy boughs,
Strong in their voice and youth,
And between their songs we made our vows
With a kiss to seal their truth;
And I turn'd to you as I said, "This stream"—
The stream was then so sweet—
"Has music fit for our coming dream,"
And the red leaf fell at our feet.

The blushes lay warm on your gentle cheek,

As I took your hand in mine,
While your eyes they could not, would not speak
Aught but that love of thine;
And you smiled as I clasp'd and kiss'd you still—
Your smile was then so sweet—
But ever between the joy and thrill
The red leaf fell at our feet.

I took the curls of your long, rich hair,
And nursed them in my hand,
As we laid in the future clear and fair,
The dreams we both had plann'd;
We had nothing to do with life's alloy—
O the heart will rise and beat—
But still as we spoke of our coming joy
The read leaf fell at our feet.

We stood by the gate as the virgin night
Set her footsteps on the hill,
Yet so sweet were your eyes with their dark rich light
That I fondly linger'd still;
But hours wait not whatever we do—
And lovers' hours are sweet—
So I kiss'd you again and said, "Be true,"
And the red leaf lay at our feet.

Now I walk this life with a solemn brow,
For the sweetest of hopes is fled,
And the blossoms that once would burst and blow
Are now for ever dead.
Yet I smile as they question "Why is this?"—
O the pain of the inward heat!—
And seem to be gay as I laugh and say,
The red leaf fell at our feet.

HE CAME FROM A LAND

He came from a land whose shadows
Were brighter than our day;
And he sang of the streams and meadows,
And then he went away.

Now I turn from the heart that ever
Will moan for the clay behind;
When the soul is such glorious liver
In the boundless realms of mind.

So at night when the shadows grow dreary,
And a sorrow is in my breast,
And the wings of life grow weary,
And flutter as if for rest:

Then I open my little book-case,
When the quiet is breathing low,
And I take from the shelf in silence
A volume of long ago.

And I read and read by the firelight,
Till quick and clear as chimes
The man himself is with me,
And is talking to me in rhymes:

Talking of waving meadows
And cunningly-hidden brooks,
With the quietest gush of eddies
That the flowers may see their looks:

Babbling of summer and sunshine,
And hills that reach the cloud;
And this—all this in whispers,
For he never speaks aloud.

Then betimes when I shut the volume
To walk in the quiet street,
When the stars, which are shadows of angels,
Have made the silence sweet:

He follows me still like a presence
That none but spirits see;
And at every pause of my footstep
His music is speaking to me:

Whispers and speaks till the night-time
So trembles with all its tone
That I cannot but let my being
Move into the clasp of his own.

So whenever I lift the volume,
Like summer-beams that glow,
That spirit comes out from the silence
And babbles of long ago.

A PARTING

The sunlight fell through the shadowy trees
In smiles all soft and sweet,
While the incense breath of an early breeze
Stirr'd the primrose at our feet.

And you stoop'd to pluck its round bright eye
That peep'd up to the day,
Then turn'd from its golden bloom with a sigh,
For your thoughts were far away.

Ay, far away with some dearer one,
And hearing within your ear,
Breath'd out in love's low undertone
The vows that you loved to hear.

I knew I had no share in your heart,
And yet I could but speak,
While my life's sweet thoughts began to start
With the blush upon your cheek.

But you whisper'd as light as a leaf when turn'd
By the breath of the wooing wind,
A low sweet whisper, as if it mourn'd
For the pain it left behind.

And your eyes for a moment met my own
With the love that might have been,
Then slowly sank, and their light was gone,
And the sunlight fell between.

Ah me! through that sunlight I see thee now,
With the old-love-bloom on your cheek,
And within your eyes the same sweet glow
Of the thoughts you would not speak.

Then my heart, like a pilgrim, makes its choice,
And flings all thoughts away,
And listens again to thy low sweet voice,
As thine own did to his that day.

WHERE I AM LYING NOW

The first sweet wind of the summer
Is breathing upon my cheek,

And swaying the heads of the grasses
That throb with a wish to speak.
The spray is upon the hawthorn,
The leaf is out on the bough,
The light swift birds
Are singing sweet words
Where I am lying now.

My head is upon a primrose,
My hand on a violet,
My foot has bent down a daisy—
It is looking up at me yet.
Two butterflies—one like snow-drift,
The other like blood, I trow—
Dip their fairy hues
In the earth's sweet dews,
Where I am lying now.

I turn away from the sunlight
That is falling soft and rife,
And I hear the angel's spreading
The miraculous network of life.
And still, as their hands are plying,
They murmur a tender vow—
From heaven to earth
It is one great birth—
Where I am lying now.

O, dweller within the city,
Come forth from its smoke and dust,
And, were it but one hour only,
Clean thy soul from its growing rust.
Here stretch thyself on this couch of grass,
With a hand upon thy brow,
And take a part,
With a poet's heart,
In the dreams I am dreaming now.

A MEMORY

As soft as an autumn leaf will light
When the winds are hush'd and still,
Fell your hand into mine that summer night,
When the moon rose above the hill.

And silent and pale through the holy skies

Rose she on her starry throne;
But I turn'd from her beams to your own sweet eyes,
That were looking up to, my own—

Looking up to my own, dear love,
With their sweetest and tenderest glow,
As the angels may look from their home above
On their kindred types below.

And I saw in their depths, like some glorious balm,
All the wealth of their loving lore;
And the thoughts in my breast grew into calm,
That were restless an hour before;

And the earth had a brighter look for me,
For I saw with other eyes,
And a whisper rose up like some symphony
Spirit-sung in paradise.

And beneath that whisper we stood nor stirr'd,
The silence was so divine;
While our hearts, not our lips, spoke their own sweet word,
And your eyes look'd up to mine.

O night! that now like a star is seen
In the past's ever golden sky,
Come back with the joy and the thrill that have been,
And that dear love-melody.

And it comes again with its magic tone,
And the stars come out to teach,
And your hand falls as light as a leaf in my own,
And our eyes look into each.

Then the thoughts that are restless in my breast
Grow as still as still may be;
And my heart feels the calm of thine own sweet rest,
And that dear love-melody.

So whenever my life will droop and pine,
And my thoughts rush to and fro,
Then I dream that your hand slips into mine
As it did in the long ago.

AGNES

Open again the garden door,
When the flowers live their little time,
And I stand as you used to stand before
By the rose-bush in its prime.

And I pluck one bud from the laden stem—
This is for you I say;
Then I take a leaf from the glowing gem,
And fling the rest away.

Now why should I place this single leaf
Where my other treasures lie?
And why should I keep it like the grief
That is seen in a thoughtful eye?

I keep it because it was thus you stood,
That golden afternoon,
Plucking a rose in your maiden mood,
And humming a low, sweet tune:

Humming a low, sweet tune alone,
And watching, with half a smile,
The fairy rose-leaves that were strewn
Around your feet the while.

And I stood in the shade of the garden door,
And heard you at your song,
And saw the rich leaves downward pour
As the low winds came along.

Now, when death has pluck'd your life's sweet bud,
And your footsteps are heard no more,
I think it a joy to stand where you stood,
By the rose at the garden door.

So I creep in as beneath some fear
And pluck with trembling hand
A rose from the bush you held so dear
Ere you went to the spirit land.

And I take one leaf from the bud—no more—
Then fling the rest away,
And turn again to the garden door
In the golden summer day.

And I whisper, "The bud that I resign
Is thy clay to its own earth given;
But the leaf that I keep is that spirit of thine,

With its incense—all of Heaven."

MARY

Roses fade, and why not you?
Mary, in whose eyes we view
Sweetest fancies peeping through,

So that unto us they seem
Colours in a fairy's dream—
Shaded pool of woodland stream,

Where the rounded pebbles lie,
Underneath its melody:
Thus within thine earnest eye

All the happy thoughts we see
Rise in their sweet purity,
Speaking evermore of thee.

Roses fade, but thy decay
Must be very far away;
Angels live more than a day:

Yet if thou shouldst link thy fate
To the rose's blushing state,
Thou canst never shame thy mate.

Like the rose, if Death should come
And bear thee to his silent home,
Where thy kindred spirits roam,

Thou shalt leave, as a relief
Behind thee, calming down our grief,
All the fragrance of its leaf:

Thus within our hearts shall be,
For ever as a type of thee,
The incense of thy memory.

THE WORSHIP OF SORROW

He who, in his young sweet life-time,
When his heart with its visions was rife,

Hath felt not the worship of sorrow
Lapping round the shores of that life:

Goes out to the toil of his fellows
With no share in their hopes or their fears;
And can only stand at a distance
And see them weep their tears.

Nor hath he found out in the night-time,
When his heart and himself were alone,
That each wondrous chord in their bosom
Was an unseen link to his own,

And that every yearning within them,
The manifold aim and desire,
Came along that link, as the message
Is spoken in shocks through the wire.

It was thus in that past existence,
With its purposeless unrest,
When the infinite nature of sorrow
Was clasping me breast to breast.

And I stood in the dim, hush'd twilight,
While the rising tears made me blind,
As within, like a rain-quicken'd streamlet;
Rose the hopes and fears of my kind.

I am now in my bearded manhood,
And the finer perceptions then
Have roughen'd and dull'd in their feelings,
Since I stood with my shoulder to men.

But still at stray times, when the labour
And fret of the day is o'er,
That early worship comes backward,
As a wave returns to the shore.

It comes when I stand in the silence
On the bridge at the head of the town,
With the streamlet running beneath me,
And the stars above looking down.

But most when I go to the city,
And see upon either side
The restless hurry of faces
That come and go like the tide.

For I know that each one in his bosom,
Amid the toil and the din,
Has a goal set out in the future
Which he braces himself to will.

And I also know, ere the struggle
And the life-long conflict be o'er,
He must enter this temple of sorrow,
And worship, weary and sore.

For this mystical life around us,
Like the earth, with its day and night,
Is a hope and a fear and a sorrow,
Till we enter the purer light.

EARLY POET LIFE

How bright were those early summers
When, like Heaven's own dazzling bow,
All the rapt, deep life of the poet
Rose up with its wildest glow.

When the quick, sweet rush of the fancy
Came on me like a fairy crowd,
Or a sudden gush of sunlight
Through the rift of an April cloud.

Then my heart took a deeper motion,
As from stream and hill and tree
Came a music that bore in its cadence
The sweetest of dreams to me.

Whispers, too, as when swaying grasses
Bow down to the evening wind,
Were for ever thrilling my being
With the touch of the wider mind.

Then the years that lay out before me
Rose up in their height sublime,
Giving forth in oracular voices
The promise of golden rhyme.

And my spirit at such sweet promise
Leapt up in its wild delight,
Like the North light laying its fingers
On the lips of the stars by night.

Nature wept in divinest secret
The sweetest of tears on me,
Till I lost myself in the splendour
Of the boundless good to be.

O, how bright were those early summers!
Never come such moments now;
All that early madness has faded
To a duller and paler glow.

Yet at times, like a flash of sunlight,
From the inmost depths of the heart,
The old, sweet yearnings spring upward,
That for want of words must depart.

But I whisper, "A greater triumph
Is yet to be had with thy peers
Than the one that is cool'd with the laurel,
Or a life in the front of the years.

Thou canst teach them in what of music
Is left from that early song,
All the force that lies hid in their labour
Like a saint's when his spirit is strong.

Thou canst teach them, too, that for ever,
Like the waves that come again,
So over the world's rough bosom
Flow the toiling races of men:

Who, in all their fighting and striving,
With hearts that bid them be brave,
Are as types of the soul's high wrestle
For other goals than the grave.

Yet, whatever thou sing, let thy lyrics
Have something in them of cheer,
And a battle-word for the feeble
Who sicken and weary here.

If thou sing not to them as they struggle,
With the purpose of making them strong,
Then thou thyself art a traitor
In the federation of song.

But if there be heard in thy music
The fire and the true sphere tone,

That, striking within their bosoms,
Makes a march to help them on:

Then sing with thy back to those summers,
And the wild quick flush of that time,
When thy heart had no thought of its fellows
Or the sacred priesthood of rhyme."

THE LOST EDEN FOUND AGAIN

The angels look'd up into God's own eyes,
As He shut the gateways of Paradise;

For they heard coming up from the earth below
A wail as of mortals in deepest woe;

And bending their far keen vision down,
Saw two on the earth from whom hope had flown.

Then the foremost one of the Angels said,
Drooping his wings and bowing his head—

"Here, Father, are two in Thy shape and ours
Who have lost the light of their bridal bowers,

And wander, blind in their tears, and tost
With the thoughts of their Eden for ever lost."

Then God said, turning His face on him—
"Look once again, for thine eyes are dim."

Then the Angel look'd, and, lo! he could see
A smiling Babe on the woman's knee.

While the man bent down, and within his eyes
Was the light of his former Paradise.

Then the Angel whisper'd—"My fears were vain,
For man has found his lost Eden again."

OVER THE SEA, ANNIE

The wings of the dear old past, Annie,
Are falling over me,

And again my thoughts take their flight, Annie,
Over the sea to thee.
Over the sea, over the sea,
To that quaint, gray, quiet town,
Where you walk in the evening light, Annie,
As the golden sun sinks down.

And later, when twilight begins, Annie,
And the shadows grow deep and long,
Like whispers of spirits in dreams, Annie,
I hear you singing my song—
Singing my song, and the old sweet words,
Like incense of angels rise;
And their music is in my heart, Annie,
While the tears are in my eyes.

O! just to see you again, Annie,
To walk with your hand in mine;
To stand by your side and look, Annie,
Into those eyes of thine—
Into the thoughts and the depths of those eyes,
As I did two years ago,
When we stood by the old gray tower, Annie,
With the woods and the fields below.

But the wish sinks away as it forms, Annie,
Only from over the sea,
When the twilight is coming down, Annie,
You are singing that song to me—
Singing that song, and the dear old words,
Like the incense of angels rise,
And their music is in my heart, Annie,
While the tears are in my eyes.

SONNETS TO A FRIEND

I

We part: great London with its mighty rush
Of life will daily send its shocks through thine,
As tides go up a river, but on mine
The quiet hamlet with its quiet hush
Will fall like murmurs in the night.   But still,
When the low ebbs are with us, shall we not
Dream the fair dreams of many a pleasant spot,
By which we wander'd with a happy will!

I know that all between the roaring trains,
When their wild thunder sinks, that I shall hear
The murmur of the Rhine within my ear—
All soft and tremulously sweet, like strains
Sung by some fair witch-maiden, ere the moon
Touches a mountain that will hide her soon.

II

And with the murmur of the Rhine will come
Those legends which have flung, as from a sky
We cannot see but with the inner eye,
A light that rests as in its chosen home,
On hill, and peak, and old gray towers that stand
Like sentinels to guard the rear of Time;
For he, too, lingers in that fairy clime,
And turns the glass with an unwilling hand.
Sweet Rolandseck and sweeter Drachenfels
Shall be with me, and glimpses of the vine
Big with the purple promise of the wine;
Bingen, whereon the sloping sunshine dwells;
The Lorelei rock, whose echoes still prolong
The moonlight witchery of Heine's song.

III

Through these the town of Rubens shall arise,
Its stone arms clasping the cathedral, where
His dead Christ sends a worship through the air,
And takes the daily light from out the eyes
Of those that look in awe; for there they see
Divinity as death, and woman's hands
Clasping his feet as tender as can be;
While all behind the gazer as he stands,
Devotion bends the knee in that rich light
Which flings a noonday twilight all around,
That trembles as the organ lifts again
To fretted roof that narrows to the sight,
Its unseen wailing hands of holy sound
In moaning benedictions over men.

IV

The sunshine over Brussels will be mine,
But for a moment ere it pales its hue,
And slowly deepens into one grim sign
Of thunder on the field of Waterloo.
The lower thunderbolts of men have spent
The death-doom of their anger there, the plough
Follows the mission of the sword that lent
A red strength to the soil it cleaves.   And now
There will be golden harvest.   Nature craves
No boon from men.   She only needs one spring
To work her miracles, which, ere it pass,
Has woven in the joy of fashioning,
Over a battle-field and dead men's graves,
The green forgetfulness of growing grass.

V

And quiet Weimar, hush'd of look and staid,
As if she knew the passing stranger came,
Drawn to her by the splendour and the fame
Of her two mighty sons, whose dust is laid
Within her bosom side by side.   And she
Covers their ashes still with flowers that bind
Mortals to all the high Immortals.   He,
Goethe—a sea without one waft of wind;
Schiller—the river yearning for that sea,
High, pure and restless, with an upward mind.
So let her keep their sacred dust.   For through
The march of ages as they sweep along,
Will rise the potent voices of these two—
The ocean and the river of her song.

VI

And thou, in such calm moments, wilt again
Stand in that holy silent light which swims
With unsung liturgies and incensed hymns
That ever teach us life is light and vain!
Nay, in thy spirit thou wilt walk in awe
Adown the column'd vista of the nave,
Till transept, altar, and high architrave
Deepen and take the universal law
Of worship. Or wilt thou become as one

Who hath no motion, and with eyes that seem
To gaze beyond their light, drink in the mild
Celestial splendour of our Raphael's dream,
And steep'd in all the art thou gazest on—
Half worship the Madonna and her Child!

VII

Half worship?   Nay, full worship must be thine,
For all the best of Raphael's soul is there,
Glowing as in that hour when the divine
Vision was with him, and the very air
Was wavy with that glory which we now
See crowning, with a splendour fair and mild,
The Virgin Mother as she clasps the Child
And smiling, for the sweetness on her brow
Is of that other light the painter saw
In those high moments when his glorious art
Lay round him like a heaven.   We turn away
Breathing the spell of some unconscious awe,
And, turning, keep that sweetness in our heart
That mingles not with that of common day.

VIII

Or Guido, where beneath the crown of thorns
Love haloes the divinest of all eyes,
And struggles with despair with unheard sighs,
Conquers, and in conquering ever mourns
Behold the man!   But thou canst never reach,
Even with thy spirit's purest touch,
That sorrow, or enfold in thy frail speech
The earnest sad divinity of such.
Thou seest only as through tears, the dread
Shadow of that agony of pain,
And those grand eyes that ever look above
With that far yearning, till, from overhead,
God stoops and slowly arches in the twain,
The unfading glory of unconquer'd love.

IX

I know thou wilt.   And so to me the past

Is richer from my pleasant days with thee,
And wears a happy memory to me,
Chat, though the years may dim and die, will last.
We were not as we said with jest and smile,
"Two idle dreamers of an empty day;"
The future takes its colour and display
From what is best within us.   So the while
There might be rising to the inner ken
The larger nature which must come with thought
Grown wider from a wider view of earth,
And earnest purposes to shape our lot
To all the grander things that take their birth
Wherever God reveals Himself to men.

Alexander Anderson – A Concise Bibliography

A Song of Labour & Other Poems (1873)
The Two Angels & Other Poems (1875)
Songs of the Rail (1878)
Ballads and Sonnets (1879)
Later Poems (1912)